Talking abc

to

your

adopted

child

Prue Chennells and

Marjorie Morrison

Published by
British Agencies for Adoption & Fostering
(BAAF)
Skyline House
200 Union Street
London SE1 0LX

Charity registration 275689

First published 1995
Second edition 1998
© BAAF 1998

British Library Cataloguing in Publication Data
A catalogue reference record for this book is available from the
British Library

ISBN 1 873868 55 3

Illustrations by Sarah Rawlings
Designed by Andrew Haig & Associates
Typeset by Ian Hawkins
Printed and bound by Stanley L Hunt Ltd

Contents

Acknowledgements

This is the second edition of *Talking About Adoption to Your Adopted Child* and is based on a previous edition published in 1995. Both editions, in turn, were based on a previous book titled *Explaining Adoption to Your Adopted Child*, authored by Prue Chennells.

This edition has been updated and revised by Marjorie Morrison, Child Placement Consultant, BAAF Scotland and takes account of any significant legislative changes in England and Wales and in Scotland.

We would like to thank the following people for all their suggestions and advice in the preparation of this edition including reading and commenting on the script, rewriting sections or preparing new material, and preparing text for production: Hedi Argent, Susanne Clarke, Marilene Flight, Philly Morrall, Phillida Sawbridge, Shaila Shah, Marcia Spencer, Stephanie Stone, Ann Sutton and Lesley Watson.

Finally, this book could not have been written without the wholehearted collaboration of many adopted people and adoptive parents who generously shared their experiences.

1

Why talking with your child is so important

Like many adopted people, I found my adoption papers whilst looking in the "deed box"; my birth mother's first name I never forgot, although every other detail became a blur. I knew I could not discuss this with my mother because it had always been a taboo subject; her answer used to be 'If you loved me you wouldn't ask'. I was 12 years old when I found the adoption papers, just after my father died.

Whether you have just become an adoptive parent or whether you have been one for years, you will know that one of the most important things about adoption is what your child understands about it as a part of his or her life history. If you are worried about talking to your child, we hope that this book – which has been based on the personal experiences of many adopted people and many adopters – will help to make it easier for you.

Nowadays, all kinds of children are adopted – babies, toddlers, school-age children, even teenagers. Coming from many different backgrounds and cultures, some of these children may have lived with their birth parents for a considerable period while others may have no memories of their birth families. All, of course, have their own individual and unique personalities, many show the effects of emotional hurt and damage, and some have additional needs resulting from physical or learning disabilities.

I did not know I was adopted until at the age of 12 it could no longer be kept secret. During our first week at High School we were asked to bring along our birth certificates as proof of our ages. This request threw my mother into a panic; she said she would have to try and find mine. Later the other girls took turns to trot to the front of the class to show the long pink certificates to the teacher. Come my turn and I made an excuse to leave the room and there in the corridor stood my parents earnestly talking to the headmistress. I remember feeling sick and I knew I was going to be expelled as I had not produced my birth certificate. The four of us stood like a tableau looking at one another.

The headmistress said to my parents, 'I think you should tell her as soon as possible'. Tell me what? I had to wait until I arrived home at 4.30pm, by which time I was trembling with apprehension and unable to eat any tea. Mother silently handed me a small, pink square. A birth certificate? Not mine surely? The date of birth was mine, the surname was mine too, but who on earth was this female?

For some children placed as babies or toddlers, talking about their adoption is about helping to develop their understanding of their place in their adoptive family, the decisions already made on their behalf by caring adults, and piecing together a life history which is not in their conscious memory. For older children, talking about adoption may start at a very different point; they may already be very aware of the circumstances surrounding their separation from their birth parents and be seeing adoption as a way of securing their future through a plan they may have been actively involved in making. Regardless of the starting point, talking about adoption is about developing healthy ways of including understanding and knowledge of birth family and origins within the security of the experience of being part of an adoptive family. Some adopters find it helps to think of the child's birth family like an extension of the adoptive family; it is not a conflict between "our" or "your" child but an understanding of a joint concern for the well-being of "their" child with full recognition of the importance of both the birth and adoptive parents. We hope that, whatever your circumstances, you will find some useful information here.

Why do children need to know all this?

Everyone has the right to know about their own history and most people, sooner or later, feel a deep need to know about it. What are their roots? Where did they get their physical characteristics from – the colour of their hair, their height, their weight? What combination of inherited characteristics, individual qualities and life experiences has made them the people they are? Try thinking back to the questions about your family that you had as a child – the comments, comparisons with relations and bits of "folklore" that contributed to your views of your family.

People who live within their birth family have all this history and knowledge available to them and it is easy to take it for granted. Recognising the importance of this for adopted children and adults does not minimise the value of adoptive parenthood. Learning about healthy relationships, developing a secure base from which to explore the wider world, establishing lasting values, building self-esteem based on acceptance and "unconditional love" all happen within adoptive families and are vital parts of creating adults with a strong sense of their own identity. However, adoptive parents have the added responsibility of integrating knowledge of the child's other family who gave him or her life and adopted people have the right to know their history.

The strongest relationships are based on truth – adopters and adopted people have both realised this for many years and laws have been passed to support it, allowing adopted people to see their original birth certificates at the age of 16 (Scotland) or 18 (England, Wales and Northern Ireland). This, of course, means that an adopted person who has his or her full birth certificate and is aware of his or her adoption can obtain at least minimal information about his or her birth parents. In reality, of course, even if they are not told by their adopters, most children have found out long before this: perhaps from an overheard conversation between adults who know (relatives, teachers, doctors), or a comment or taunt at school that they don't look like their parents, or the chance finding of a document at home,

> I knew I was adopted from a very early age, and that it had been a private adoption arranged by my adoptive mother's GP, following the termination on medical grounds of her own pregnancy. When I was about nine, while searching through my parents' wardrobe for hidden Christmas presents, I came across a birth certificate giving my natural mother's name, my own name at birth, and her address at the time of my birth, along with my certificate of entry in the Adopted Children's Register. I read my birth certificate but felt such guilt at finding it, instinctively knowing that my adoptive mother would not have wanted me to see it, that I quickly put it back and never mentioned that I had found it.

or, perhaps worst of all, from a thoughtless remark during a family row. Some adopters have pointed out that there is a greater tendency now for adults to talk in front of children or include them in adult conversation, and as one said, 'We feel it is really a child's right to have any information about himself or herself before anyone else has it.' Experiences of finding out unexpectedly at a later age can leave a lasting scar upon children and adults and can damage their relationship with the adoptive parent – sometimes permanently. People who discover suddenly that a loved parent is not, after all, a blood relation have their faith and trust in that parent shattered. The relationship will never be the same again. Whereas those children who have grown up secure in the knowledge that they are adopted, and know that they are loved and valued, have a relationship with their adoptive parents built on honesty and trust.

What if I don't want to tell my child?

If you are worried about talking to your child and wish you could avoid it, please do take time to talk this over and think about the implications for the future. Being worried or concerned about talking about this subject is common to many adoptive parents – just as many parents, when considering discussing any sensitive subject, are anxious about approaching it in the right way.

The starting point, of course, is to be convinced that you are doing the right thing. Some adoptive parents feel they want to "protect" their children. If you have doubts about this, the best people to hear from are adopted adults. Those who were not told by their parents but found out themselves have said things like, 'It wasn't so much that I was adopted that shattered me, more the fact that my mum and dad had been deceiving me for years'. Many adopted adults now benefit from being part of self-help groups – and sadness has been expressed by a number that they had so many questions to ask, and they knew sometimes that their adoptive parents had more information but they just could not bridge the gap and talk about it.

Some adoptive parents, being honest with themselves, recognise that part of not wanting to tell their children is the feelings it arouses in themselves. Realising this and knowing what the feelings are about is a major hurdle. It is time well spent to talk this through first so that upset feelings about adult concerns are not transferred to your child. Often couples can support each other in this, or individuals or couples can seek outside advice or counselling. If your anxieties then are about how to approach your child, we hope this book will help.

We now know a lot more about what children need at different stages of their development. Whether your initial hurdle is introducing 'adoption' as a subject you can talk about with your child, or you are adjusting to an older child's entry to your family with perhaps some very strong views and feelings about what has already happened to him or her, the anxieties and concerns are likely to be around the complexity of discussing all sorts of sensitive information about the child's birth family and earlier experiences. What we have included here is based on what we have learnt from those who have already faced this.

A question commonly asked of adopted people is: 'How did you feel when you found out you were adopted?' It is a question I cannot answer. I never 'found out' I was adopted, it was just a fact I had known all my life. I must have been told of my adoption by the time I was three years old, and simply grew up with the knowledge. I was greatly loved, wanted and, as I was keen to tell playground adversaries, chosen. I was told I was adopted as the lady I was born to was unable to look after me. As it was only illness that prevented mummy from looking after me, I assumed my natural mother had been ill. I equated illness with old age, and throughout my childhood visualised Roz, my natural mother, as a small, bent, old lady in a grey coat and felt hat.

Starting to talk about adoption

I usually chose the time when she was wrapped in her towel and lying on the mat after her bath – a nice secure time. Obviously it wasn't every bath time but as she learned to talk she would ask me at this particular time to tell her about my visits to the foster home to see her and 'what did we all say?' She, like many children, likes repetition – it seems to give security – and at first it was like another fairy tale for her. Now it's a reality, and a pleasant one.

Adoption today is a much more open subject. Although far fewer babies are placed for adoption nowadays, there are thousands and thousands of adopted children and adults in Britain. Families vary considerably with very many children experiencing the separation or divorce of parents, forming new relationships with step-parents or spending at least part of their childhood with a single parent. We know all these areas are discussed much more openly now including directly with the children concerned. This, however, does not automatically make it easier for adoptive parents to feel comfortable in approaching discussion of something which is so close to the heart of their family life.

Adoptive parents too are very aware that what starts off simply as telling a child they are adopted is the beginning of helping their child understand his or her place in the adoptive family and integrating into this their knowledge of their birth family. This first step needs careful consideration; it will set the scene for later discussions as what the child needs to understand will change and increase at different stages of development. If you simply talk about your child's adoption in a matter-of-fact, down-to-earth way, your child will accept it in the same way. On the other hand, if you think of it as something which is difficult and embarrassing to talk about, your child will feel the same. Talking to other adoptive parents and perhaps rehearsing some simple words can help you feel more comfortable. Don't forget that it is up to you to bring the subject up; don't wait for the child to do it. A comment made by an adopted teenager illustrates this well: 'My adoptive parents have always been very open about everything connected with my adoption and were ready to answer any of my questions. I sadly have not had the courage to ask all I would have liked to.' Children can feel just as awkward as adults and be less equipped to find the right words to help them ask.

If you convey a positive sense of adoption to your child and he or she grows up with the knowledge that being adopted is a good thing, that firm base will stand your child in good stead as years go by. Whatever your child's age, warmth and affection are very important ingredients in sharing information.

If your child was placed as a baby

If you adopted your child when he or she was very young, you can start your explaining at a very early age. The fact that your child is adopted will be just another fact to be taken in along with all the other information being learned. Your child will not understand what adoption means, but will become familiar with

What to call the birth parents

We have used the term "birth parent" to describe the child's biological parent. What term you use is up to you: "first parent" is one possibility, and can also be used to describe divorced parents of your children's friends, thus showing that plenty of other children have "first" mums and dads. Other adopters have pointed out that they avoided "new" mummy and daddy for themselves as it sounded like a replacement and they wanted all parties to have their place and be valued. For very young children, "tummy mummy" sums it up very well. Some adopters prefer to use first names: 'Well, you grew in Elizabeth's tummy and then you came to mummy and daddy.' For obvious reasons, the term "real parent", to describe the birth parent, is not a good choice as it may make you appear less "real".

the term as something positive. But do not feel that you have to stress adoption all the time. If you keep dwelling on the fact that adoption is special and different you may find your child expects special treatment! A very few simple facts are enough here just to set the foundation that your child is adopted and had other "first" parents before coming to live with you. Some people use commercially available books as bedtime stories to introduce the idea; others prefer to start making the child's own personal book themselves.

If your child joined you as a toddler

Toddlers are too young to understand what adoption means or to have enough language ability to tell you what they are thinking or feeling. However, the placement of a toddler always needs careful planning as they are certainly aware of being moved. Toddlers can find this a very difficult and distressing time and need a lot of help and support from both the foster carers they may have been with, and their new adoptive parents. Part of this often involves finding very concrete ways to help them understand that the adoptive family is where they will be staying and establishing their long-term security. Actions and words need to go along hand-in-hand and this includes "adoption". Photographs of the introduction period, and, in some instances, visits back to the foster carers can be natural prompts for confirming the information given and finding out if the child needs to ask any more questions. There are a few children's books which can help in opening up discussion about adoption (see Useful Books).

Introducing adoption to older children

Adoption is not just about babies; nowadays children who have reached school-age are adopted. Sometimes this is by their current foster carers. If you are a foster carer in this position you will already have been actively involved in helping the child make sense of what has happened to him or her so far. You may know his or her birth parents through access visits and may have supported the child through some very difficult periods. The possibility of adoption is something which may grow naturally out of this if it becomes clear that the child is unable to return to his or her birth parents. However, both the timing and manner of introducing the idea of adoption may need careful planning. There will be agency procedures to go through to change from being foster carers to adopters, and also the legal process may be quite prolonged especially if the birth parents do not agree to the adoption.

While many children are relieved at being offered the security of adoption or are desperate to be claimed, the possibility of this change can bring conflicting feelings to the surface. It is often important in introducing adoption in these circumstances not to put the child into the position of "choosing". Use of techniques like the three circles for birth parent, legal parent and parenting parent can help children see that their birth parents still have a place in their lives, even if legal responsibility for them changes.

Aspects of parenting

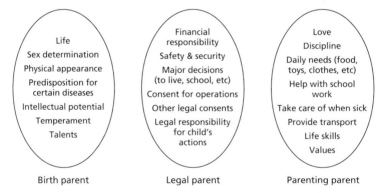

The above figure is taken from *A Child's Journey through Placement* by Vera Fahlberg (BAAF, 1994)

Such ideas can also help foster carers introduce the idea of adoption to children they are preparing to move on. The timing of any discussion of adoption is very important as it can raise such high hopes and expectations. A foster carer needs to work very closely with a child's social worker to try and avoid a situation where children remain in limbo or lose confidence or self-esteem if an adoptive family is not found quickly.

For new adoptive parents, meeting a well-prepared older child can be quite overwhelming, particularly if the child immediately "claims" you! If you are in that position, as well as finding out all about the child's background, it is important to know just what they have been told and look at a few possible scenarios of the first meeting. Otherwise you may be catapulted into talking about adopting the child while you are all still "testing the waters". On the other hand, many such placements do include a prolonged period of fostering prior to adoption.

It takes sensitivity to realise when it is right for everyone to lodge the adoption application in the court, in Scotland an adoption petition. This is an important and significant step in a growing relationship and the court will also take into account your child's views and wishes depending on his or her age and under-standing. In Scotland, children aged 12 or over need to sign their own agreement to their adoption. Introducing the decision to adopt includes steps that are very clear and visible to the child such as the visit of the guardian *ad litem*, in Scotland the curator *ad litem*, and can precipitate fresh talk about thoughts and feelings that may have lain dormant or are linked to a new phase in your child's development.

3

What information do you need?

It's essential to be absolutely honest. You mustn't tell them anything that isn't true or leave out anything important. By the time our kids are grown up they will probably be able to see their own social services records and if they find out that we've been in any way untruthful they'll never trust us again.

Nowadays adoption agencies are required by law to give you, the adoptive parent, written information about your child's background. It is up to you, too, to ask questions. Find out as much as you can about your child's birth parents – their family history, their jobs, their medical history, their physical characteristics. Knowledge about things like height and build will come in useful the day your child asks questions like: 'How come I'm so tall/short/fat/thin?' And you really need medical information to be able to answer questions like: 'Any family history of asthma/eczema/heart disease?' at the doctor's. Your child may turn out to be particularly keen on music, or sport, or mathematics, and it would be useful to be able to say, 'Well, your mother/father was a musician/dancer/footballer/ engineer, etc'. Anything you can find out will be valuable, but you may find you have to keep asking. The social workers who have worked with your child's birth parent(s) could have information that may not seem important to them but could be vital to your child.

However, no list of questions can be complete. For example, adopters, when asked, can be very satisfied with all the medical information they receive – yet still be prompted to come back with fresh questions springing from media publicity about new medical advances indicating predispositions to certain conditions in biological families. So perhaps the most important piece of information is about ways to find out answers to new questions in the future.

It is really crucial that you write down anything you find out. You might think you will remember, but you might not need some of this information for 10 or 15 years and your memory may not be so good then! When you do need it, you will find that having all

> **It's been a gentle revealing of facts over the years, sometimes softening the truth but never avoiding it if it was necessary to answer the question. Our children trust us to tell them the truth as far as we are able or to try to find out the answer for them.**

the details written down will be invaluable. And obviously you will need to keep it all in a safe place.

If you adopted your child years ago and are missing this sort of information, it is still worth getting back in touch with the adoption agency to try and find out more. Social workers, foster carers and children's home staff may all remember various things and have useful facts to give you. Keeping in touch with them occasionally is a good idea and makes it easier to get further information later on. You should also think about the different sorts of written information that would be helpful.

Some questions you might ask the social worker

What day was my child born and at what time?
Was it an easy or difficult birth?
How long did my child stay with the birth mother?
Where did my child go then? (find out as much detail as possible, according to the child's age)
When did my child have his first tooth, take her first steps, say his first words, etc
Where did the birth parents' families come from?
Where were they both living when my child was born?
How old was the birth mother? And father?
What did they look like?
What did they wish for their child?
What were their likes and dislikes?
What were their hobbies and skills? Where did they work?
What sort of schools did they go to?
How did they get about (car, bike, etc)?
Does my child have any brothers or sisters?
Where are they now?

You will be able to think of other questions. Try writing a list for yourself to tick off as you get answers.

You may have information aimed at your "adult" understanding and also something written for your child. You need to discuss with your social worker at what age it is appropriate to share this. If the birth mother has written a letter, or is prepared to do so, again it helps to know how it is written, at what age it could helpfully be shared with your child, and what level of understanding your child would need in order to make best use of the information.

As many children nowadays are placed past babyhood you will, of course, need to know as much as possible about what has happened to your child since birth. It is important not to be rushed in absorbing this information and to take your time to understand what it might mean for your child.

Documents you will find useful

Written information about your child (required by law)
Photographs of your child as a baby, a toddler, etc
Photographs of your child's birth family
Any other documents or mementos of the child's birth family such as a letter from the birth mother.
Any updating information eg. through a Post Box.
A life story book about your child if one has been prepared

Often reports are written for social services departments, in Scotland social work departments, or for the courts and might not tell you all you need to know as adoptive parents. You should also be able to meet key people who have been involved in caring for your child.

For your child, the key question is likely to be: 'Why was I adopted?' The simple answer, 'Your birth mother could not look after you, and I (we) wanted a child very much, so you came to live with us,' will do for a start. But why the birth parent(s) could

In our family when one of the children has said, 'I wish I grew in your tummy, mum', I have said, 'Well, I would have liked to grow babies in my tummy but if I had it wouldn't have been you and you would have been given to a different mummy and daddy, so I think it's better as it is'.

not manage will need explaining in more detail as the child gets older. Sometimes the initially less problematic backgrounds can be tricky in this respect. Now that so many single parents keep their children, those who appear capable people but choose to place their child for adoption can be harder for the child to understand. Some children are particularly sensitive to the thought of rejection, that they were not wanted, or that somehow if their birth parent was "OK" then he or she must have been a "bad" child. This is where it pays off for you to spend some time understanding as much as possible the reasons for the birth parent's decision.

Of course many children now placed for adoption have very complex and problematic backgrounds. Some explanation of this is the response to the question wanting to know why they were adopted. But as an adoptive parent you also need to consider how you share distressing facts. However many times you have talked with your child about why he or she was adopted, it is likely to be the starting point for many more discussions, so you will need to feel confident that you have come to grips with all the information that is available. See p.33 for further discussion of this subject.

Now that openness is more a feature of adoption, there may be

We always had a very positive attitude towards adoption but there was something missing until we got the opportunity to write once a year to our daughter's birth mother. We now know that she receives our letters and photographs, that she appreciates them and that she is happy with the situation. I think I understand better now about the missing piece of a child's life if she has no information about her birth parents or the circumstances surrounding her birth and subsequent adoption. I, too, felt it...there was a person out there somewhere who had given life to our precious daughter. I wanted to know more about her, to feel that I shared something with someone who thought and felt and was a real person, not just a name.

other ways in which you will gain very direct information about your child's birth parents. If you are adopting a baby with the birth parents' agreement, you may have the opportunity for a meeting. This will help you to talk to your child in the future as you will be able to give a very real personal description of the birth mother and/or father. They may be able to give you mementos for the child at a later date and you may also be able to take photographs which will help your child see your understanding of the importance of his or her personal history.

Some agencies offer an information exchange service so that perhaps once a year information about the child's progress and significant changes in the birth parents' life may be exchanged via a third party. This information may be particularly helpful at later stages if your child needs to find out a lot more information than you received initially.

Many adoptive parents find this a very helpful service although it also raises concerns. At what age and how do you tell your child about this? What if your child at a later stage does not want to take part? It can be very useful if, at a much later stage, an adopted young person wants to make contact with a birth parent to know their current circumstances. However, if there have been significant changes, those may affect the information already given. This could be about the birth of other children, added problems the birth parent has faced, or significant improvements in their lives. New information may not alter the reasons why your child was placed for adoption – that decision depended on circumstances at a particular time – but it may "round off" discussions about absent birth parents and perhaps guide decisions about any future contact.

For some older children, direct contact with birth parents or other members of the extended family, like grandparents or brothers and sisters, may be an agreed part of the plan. Clearly this must be negotiated carefully at the beginning so that it can work in the best interests of your child. It can combine the security of adoption, which makes it clear who the legal parent is, with a built-in recognition of the birth family and the importance of the integration of all these important people for the child.

You, the adopter, have taken on the responsibilities as well as the pleasures of being a parent to your child. One of the responsibilities is to help your child grow to be an adult secure in as much knowledge as possible about his or her past. This information is their right, and you are the best person to see that your child has it.

4

What children need at different times

We introduced things gradually to our daughter – the fact that her mother couldn't manage to look after her family of seven children satisfied her at first, but she soon wanted to know why she couldn't manage. This led to the fact that her father was away from home a lot so she had to cope alone. This again satisfied her for a while and she described her father as a "wanderer"... but gradually she wanted to know why he was away so much and we had to tell her that he sometimes stole things and got sent to prison. We tried not to imply that he was a bad man but that he took drugs and needed money to buy them. She is now strongly anti-drugs but seems to feel that people who take them are "silly" rather than "bad".

In the past, talking to children about their adoption and their family history raised questions about the impact of such information on their emotional development. We now have a lot more knowledge stemming from the work of a psychologist in the USA, David Brodzinsky, who is also himself an adoptive parent, about what children understand in terms of both their cognitive and emotional development. This makes it clear that explaining adoption is something that continues throughout childhood and into adulthood and what is needed is linked to recognised stages in children's development. Developing such a framework has made increasing sense to adoptive parents involved in the "telling". People did worry for a while that we might have swung from saying too little too late to overloading children with more knowledge than they could cope with. Some adoptive parents worried too that children who seemed quite happy about their adoption when they were younger then began bringing up questions and concerns. We now see this as a very natural stage in the development of understanding.

Just as children may at different times have a range of feelings about their adoption, adoptive parents too are likely to find a variety of emotions triggered at different stages. When you applied to adopt you probably talked about the reminders of fertility issues that can recur. Sometimes this can happen unexpectedly and catch you unawares, but it is in thinking of all the stages of talking about adoption – about your child's birth parents and why you chose to adopt – that you can predict this will come to the fore. From the young child perhaps wanting to "grow in your tummy" through the stages of curiosity and sometimes confusion about these "other" parents, the adolescent anxieties about sexuality and on to thoughts about becoming grandparents, you are likely to be doing your best to say and do what is right for your child and at the same time recognising feelings in yourself that you do not necessarily want to transfer. Where it is a couple who have adopted, this is when it is important to be able to share such feelings and support each other. Close friends and family are often helpful supports also.

| Stages in development

So, what are these stages and what do they mean for adopted children and their parents? Children develop at different speeds, so what follows is only a rough guide to the ages at which new developments occur.

First of all, small children under four years of age seldom have an intellectual understanding of adoption. However, this does not mean there is no point in introducing the idea. Children's perception develops ahead of their understanding of concepts and at this early stage they are absorbing all sorts of ideas of themselves as separate and different from others. This is a simple but growing awareness of who they are: whether they are a boy or a girl, the colour of their eyes, hair, skin, personal attributes, family roles, what mummies and daddies do, etc. These differences may have values attached to them as a result of parental connotations and the feelings that come with them. The term "adopted" can fit in here and become another difference which can have "good" or "bad" values attached. So at this early age the feelings conveyed around the words spoken are most important both in creating a positive atmosphere around adoption and also in helping children realise it is an open subject that can be talked about easily. Of course this sounds easy, but is not always that easy in practice.

For some adoptive parents this may be because they have grown so close to the child that it is hard to talk about their having "other" parents or about the fact that the child was not born to them. For others, knowing logically that at a very early age the child only needs very simple limited information does not stop them being anxious about all the more complicated background information that they are going to have to address in the future. In this situation, people often seek the "right" book to read to their child, which can certainly help. However, if you are really feeling worried it is best to sort out the reasons why first so that adult anxieties do not transmit themselves to the child. Then, once you feel comfortable about what you are doing, the most natural way for you will fall into place. This may be the use of a bedtime storybook, but for some people that seems too planned

Your child's own story

Long before your child is old enough to go to school you will be faced with questions like 'Where did I come from?' All parents are. You can answer simple, direct questions like this with simple, direct answers like 'You grew in someone else's tummy and then you came to join our family'. You can build on this by reading from relevant picture books but, best of all, tell your child's own story, which will almost certainly become a great favourite. If you don't have a life story book for your child, start to put one together. The story of 'the day mummy (and daddy) got me' can be used to convey great excitement and pleasure and can be illustrated with any details possible – like the clothes you all wore, the way you travelled, what the weather was like and what everybody concerned said. (See also 'Who is my real mummy?' in Chapter 9.)

and they prefer to build in opportunities for natural reference to the placement by looking at photographs, recalling anecdotes of first seeing their child, and so on. Many adopters find it a benefit to "practice" first, getting used to saying the words, polishing the story without being challenged, and growing comfortable with what they are saying and with acknowledging that this child is not born to them.

Once children reach the age of about four they often ask lots of questions about babies and where they come from. In fact there are lots of similarities in how children learn about adoption and about reproduction and sexual relationships. Birth and adoption are often confused in their minds. At the same time, children are widening their contacts with other adults and children

particularly through playgroups and starting school, and
perhaps talking of their adoption. Given that it is difficult to keep
fully aware of what children talk about, adoptive parents often
need to bear in mind the support available from grandparents
and other family members and close friends in confirming the
messages given about the adoption; they also need to be ready to
respond if their children meet less helpful comments. It helps to
suggest words they can use to explain to their friends what
adoption is about (you can read about what we call cover stories
in Chapter 6).

People who have adopted older children will know that it is
during these early years that many of their children's ideas and
views of themselves have their foundation. If misunderstandings
and misperceptions become established, they take a long time to
alter as the child often cannot put them into words, or finds it
too scary. The security of adoption can be hard to comprehend if
an adopted person has picked up somehow that originally they
were not wanted, maybe because they were bad or caused the
problems for their parents.

Through the school age years

From about the age of six, adopted children are likely to have
begun to understand at a simple level the meaning of adoption
and the different ways of entering a family. This is the starting
point for the child for the exploration through the years ahead
about family relationships, the permanence of adoptive
relationships, the motives both for the adoption and their birth
parents' relinquishment of them. This is not a smooth curve; it is

> There's no question of sitting down and saying 'We've
> got something to tell you'. The situation is one which is
> lived out from day to day. The facts filter through
> gradually, some in answer to questions put usually when
> you're in the middle of trying to cross a busy road or
> writing 'Happy Birthday' on a cake, and some you
> produce yourself whenever the opportunity arises.

like steps and stairs as new stages of development are reached. A significant step is around the age of eight. Young children can sometimes shock their parents by their direct way of stating concrete facts that are much more emotive to the adults. But as children mature they too begin to be more aware of the complexities. Some of this is about the permanence of the adoptive relationship with questions like, 'What if something happens to my adoptive parents?' or 'What if my birth mother's situation changes – can she come back and look for me?'. Children also begin to learn more about the needs of other people, especially the people most important to them, and may begin to wonder about their birth parents' feelings.

It is not until children are of school age that they can recognise the loss involved in adoption. It is therefore quite normal and natural that children may go through a period described by Brodzinsky as 'adaptive grieving' and for a while they may be

Aiding children's understanding

A book which looks much more fully at the different stages in children's understanding of sex, reproduction and families is *Flight of the Stork – What children think (and when) about sex and family building* by Anne C Bernstein. This is based on talking to 3–12-year-olds about how people get babies and how mothers and fathers get to be mothers and fathers. There are strong parallels between the six stages suggested by Anne Bernstein and David Brodzinsky's levels in talking about adoption. The Brodzinsky levels are included in the chapter on adoption and there are also chapters on talking with children about assisted reproduction and stepfamilies.

confused or uncertain. This can be troubling for adoptive parents who are not prepared for the possibility. The discussions about adoption that seemed so positive earlier now seem to be bringing problems. The children may become more difficult but not want to talk about it. By this stage, if children were placed when very young, there will have been many shared family experiences and adoption will seem to have found its place amongst all the normal day-to-day activities. It is not surprising therefore that adoptive parents may become worried by this change or feel that the security they had built up as parents to their child is somehow under question. Sometimes this coincides with a period when children are dealing with more questions, or even teasing at school and perhaps negative remarks about adoption. We know we cannot protect them from wider comments, but we need to be aware that these can add to a child's uncertainty and they may find it hard to share all this with their adoptive parents.Often it helps at this stage to contact one of the growing number of post-adoption counselling services either to talk through personal issues or locate an adoptive parents' self-help group. For the child, it is important to sort out the loss of the birth parent as a potential parent, but not deny him or her as a person to be integrated into the child's under-standing of himself or herself. It is obviously easier for adoptive parents to offer support if they have the opportunity to talk about their own feelings and what has been stirred up for them.

Now, more than ever, it is important for you to feel comfortable with the circumstances of your child's background and to feel sympathy and concern for the predicament which faced your child's birth parents and to begin to explain this to your child without criticising their behaviour. If children feel that their birth parents were "bad" in any way, they sometimes assume

Our daughter, adopted as a baby, loves to hear her 'own' story over and over again with different details added at each telling. Long before she could talk or possibly understand the meaning of adoption, she knew she was our 'darling adopted daughter', while her elder sister was our 'darling daughter'. She was, therefore, always aware of a difference but one that had no bearing on our love for both of them. Later, when she was able to ask about adoption, it was possible to tell her simply and naturally that her sister grew in my tummy whereas she grew in Pauline's tummy.

that this means they are bad too, or that it is their own fault their parents could not keep them. You will need to be careful with the explanations you use. If you say that the birth mother was too poor to keep your child, they may worry that you would give them up if you fell on hard times. If you say that there was no father to help, they may ask why their friends with single parents have not been given up for adoption too. You will need to balance this with an acceptance that everything in the birth family was not rosy, and that adoption was for the best. And you can build in your thankfulness and pleasure that you were able to become your child's parent.

Working this out should help the child move on to recognising their adoptive parents' "entitlement" to be their parents which comes from all the care they have given rather than the biological link. Giving careful thought to all this should provide a much more secure base of understanding for the adolescent as he or she explores the reasons for adoption that will ultimately lead to a healthy level of understanding in adulthood.

Adolescence

Adoptive parents are not alone in expressing some trepidation about a possible turbulent phase during adolescence. They do, however, have the added question: 'How much of this is due to adolescence and how much to adoption?' Adolescents have a number of common issues and concerns, for example, the competing pulls of a desire for independence with a fear of separation and finding an accepting place in the adult world; finding out more about themselves, their identity, the sort of adult they will become; dealing with emerging sexuality; concern about physical appearance; learning about forming more adult relationships and fear of rejection, and more. It certainly is not hard to see that aspects of adoption are woven through all these. If, in the middle of this, your adopted adolescent's curiosity about his or her origins reaches a peak, you may be concerned about whether more information or possibly contact with a

member of his or her birth family will help sort out the concerns
or add to the confusion.

A strong relationship based on openness and trust will certainly
help, though it may not feel like that at the time. In addition, you
may yourself need more information or contact with someone
who has access to such information and can help in teasing out
the different issues. It should help to go over old ground again
about how each one of us is unique: we all have our basic
inheritance from the people who gave us life; we all have
different life experiences, stemming from where we live and the
sort of families we grow up in; and we all have different chances
to explore and use our talents and abilities. All these things – not
just one of them – make us the people we are.

One family's experience of talking to their adopted son at
different stages of their lives is presented in the section entitled
Talking to children at different ages and stages.

Adolescents often find it easier to talk to someone other than a
parent about things that matter most to them and if this is the
case, try not to feel hurt. You may also need some independent
opportunities yourself to balance all this up and feel secure in
the vital part you have played as a parent. This could help you
wholeheartedly support his or her explorations to bring together
all these aspects of himself or herself without feeling a need to
make impossible choices. Many of the doubts, difficulties and
dilemmas which arise with adopted teenagers are part of
growing up.

Most adopted adolescents, with the support of their adoptive
parents, will find their way through this stage. Occasionally some
will need some space to sort things out and will try breaking
away from their family. As this is usually a "testing out" it is
important to "keep the door open" and often it leads to a much
more mature understanding by the young person of what they
have received from their adoptive family. Some adolescents can

benefit from meeting other young people in the same situation, and this is something which is likely to become more available, either informally through links made by their parents through self-help groups, or organised by post-adoption services that already run groups for adopted adults. Some, particularly those who were older when placed and may have had very unsettling early experiences, may need additional counselling or therapy. This is now well understood by adoption specialists who are happy to be approached about such concerns at an early stage and would not want families to be held back by anxieties that they might be "blamed" or seen as failing.

You could try returning to the agency which placed your child, contacting your local social services or social work department which may have a post-adoption support service, or finding out what post-adoption counselling services or adopters self-help groups are available locally (see Useful Organisations).

While this book is about talking about adoption to your adopted child, the evidence from the rapidly increasing use of post-adoption services is that this quest for further knowledge continues through adulthood for many adopted people. Some recent research completed by David Howe, Professor at the University of East Anglia, on the patterns of adoption shows the effects of this for a long time. Those who have a particularly stormy adolescence may not be able to tackle understanding what their adoption means for them until they are in their 20s. For example, some angry adolescents, after fighting for their independence, may reach the point of "the calm after the storm" when they can experience a more relaxed relationship. Perhaps it is only then that they can accept they were really loved and wanted. (See *Adopters on Adoption* in Useful books.)

5

Some difficulties in talking

We had to help Joanna cope with the fact that her father had sexually abused her. We started to talk about different kinds of love, about the way mummies and daddies love each other being different from the way children love parents and parents love children. We explained that some grown-ups get things muddled up and don't have the same rules as other people. We said, 'When your daddy was young his daddy loved him in the way that mummies and daddies love each other so he thought it was okay to love you like that. But that is wrong and I know it's wrong and you knew it was wrong and that's why you told your teacher.'

While this book is encouraging you to start talking about adoption very early with your child to allow for a gentle natural progress through the stages, sometimes this does not happen. What should you do if you are now feeling you should have started sooner and that just makes it more difficult?

| Starting when your child is older

As long as you are not being pushed by some urgent outside pressures, it is best to think it through carefully beforehand and not rush into things. This involves first of all discussing why you left the introduction of adoption until your child was older. If you felt that you should wait until he or she was old enough to understand you will need to explain that, and be ready to counter any impression that you did not want to tell the truth or felt it was an uncomfortable secret.

Sometimes with two adoptive parents, one partner feels ready to talk comfortably but the other is more anxious. You need to talk this out between you because one parent may be more able to take the lead. If older children feel that people held back the truth they may need to do some checking out with other trusted adults as well. If you are anxious that you might have to talk about your infertility or details about the birth parents that you are unsure about sharing, it is as well to explore in advance the sorts of words you might use that you feel you can use naturally and your child will understand.

What might be the differences in beginning telling at a later stage? First of all you cannot just slip words like adoption into more general conversation. It is not like familiarising a young child with a word that has not got a real meaning for them. An older child is likely to have come across the term adoption and may already have associated meanings and values to it. He or she will need time to explore these.

We know from adopted adults who have come together and
reflected on how they heard about their adoption, a number who
heard first in the 7-16 age range experienced a strong sense of
shock and trauma, some describing every detail of where they
were in an unforgettable way. This, of course, is about the
impact of suddenly learning such an important fact about
themselves when old enough to have some idea of what it means
– it does not mean that they have absorbed all the information
that may have been given to them. Although your child may have
reached a stage where he or she will have some understanding

It's okay to be angry

If you have been discussing something painful and your
child is angry, give them something to be angry with, for
example, a punch ball or a big cushion to kick or a
hammer and peg toy. Otherwise, they may take it out on
other children or family pets. Show them it's okay to be
angry; say things like 'I would be too if that had
happened to me – why don't you kick the cushion?' Let
them cry too. Cry with them, if you want to. And don't
feel you've dealt with it all in one conversation: come
back to the same painful subject soon, and go on
discussing it until the child doesn't need to feel so angry
any more.

of the information you are sharing, this does not mean that your
child can take it all in immediately; information will need to be
built up in stages just as if you had started earlier. Some of the
implications may be clear to your child at once but many
questions are likely to come later so that once the door is
opened, it needs to be kept open wholeheartedly and
opportunities explicitly given for further discussions.

Sometimes people feel more confident if, as well as ensuring
starting in a relaxed atmosphere when there will be privacy and
no interruptions, some of these steps are prepared, for example,
having photographs or other reminders of the first meeting, a
letter from the birth parents or the written background

information if it is appropriate to the child's age, or opportunities to talk to others like grandparents who might have shared the early days of the placement. Such possibilities, if offered, can help to reassure your child that you can be trusted to share the truth with him or her even if he or she is not ready for all of it immediately.

Telling particularly distressing facts

There are some facts that will always be very difficult to face. Your child may be the result of an incestuous union or of rape. Or possibly the necessity for adoption may have arisen because one of the birth parents abused or rejected your child; they may even be in prison as a result. Tragic episodes do occur in the lives of some young children, and if this is true of your child it will be necessary to explain what happened, although exactly what you tell and how you tell it will vary as your child grows older and has more understanding of the world.

However difficult it may be, try not to judge your child's birth parents too harshly. If your child is the result of rape or incest, it may be more helpful to your adopted child if you explain that their offending parent needed help and did not get it (see *Children of Incest: Whose secret is it?* in Useful Books).

If your child was rejected as a baby because of some disability, or was abused before being taken away from his or her parents, try to put yourself in their place. Their circumstances may have been impossible for them to cope with. Try to imagine how you would feel if you had never had a loving relationship with anyone or if you were faced with a combination of poverty, loneliness, unemployment, inadequate housing and so on: you too might be driven to breaking point. Of course, it's one thing to accept terrible facts as a mature adult, but much more difficult to convey them to a child in an acceptable way. But however inadequate you feel your child's parents may have been, there are always good points: try to find these out and emphasise them to your child. Talk about the parents in simple language the child can understand and if you can accept the facts, it will be that much easier for the child to accept them too and forgive the parents. One adopter told us, 'Children can accept anything if you tell them in the right way; it's the grown ups who find things difficult to accept.' It is also worth bearing in mind that in certain cases young people will feel better if they know that their adoptive parents do not condone the appalling behaviour of a birth parent; for example, domestic violence leading to the killing of the mother by the father is bad and must be recognised as such. What is important is that your adopted child knows that you love, trust and believe in them regardless of what has happened in their birth family.

If, however, you feel that the problem is just too big for you to handle, you might find it helpful to talk it over with another parent who has been in a similar position. Other adoptive parents may be contacted through the numerous self-help groups now established in many parts of Britain. The national adoptive parents' support organisation PPIAS (see Useful Organisations) has local organisers in most parts of Britain and also has a Resource Bank which helps families contact others

> You need to start as early as possible... by the time John (who had been battered as a baby) was two-and-a-half he knew who had hit him and where the bruises were and who'd seen them and that was why he was taken away. We said 'Well, when you were only three weeks old you used to cry a lot and your first mummy and daddy thought you were being naughty and they smacked you hard, hard enough to make very big bruises and then the nurse came and saw them and thought they shouldn't smack such a little baby so you were taken away and given to parents who wouldn't smack you. Your first mummy and daddy were very young and they didn't know that little babies aren't being naughty when they cry but cry because they're hungry and want to be cuddled.'

who have faced similar dilemmas to theirs. If you feel a trained counsellor could help you, the agency which placed your child or one of the post-adoption counselling services that are now much more widely available may be able to help (see Useful Organisations).

For some people, the most distressing fact is that they have no information to give their child. This may be because your child was abandoned as a baby. We can only imagine the distress of the mother in such circumstances but all you might have to share with the child may be a few newspaper cuttings or perhaps a piece of clothing or something left with the child. The responsibility that all adoptive parents take on of giving their child security and a sense of belonging with their whole extended family and also developing their child's personal self-confidence will be particularly important for these children who will always have a "missing piece" of their personal jigsaw (NORCAP has a subgroup for foundlings – see Useful Organisations).

If your child's adoption was contested

Your child's birth parent(s) may have wanted to keep the child, but for many different reasons may not have been allowed to. Perhaps your child had been living with you long enough to have formed a close bond which it would have been damaging to break; or perhaps the birth parents were considered unable to bring up a child adequately; or the court agreed that the risks were too great for the child to return to them. Whatever the reason, you have a delicate task ahead. While your child should not run the risk of feeling rejected like many adopted children do, he or she may go through a phase of feeling that the birth parents were treated unfairly by you as well as by the state. Your best bet is to keep showing your love for your child and your sympathy for the birth parents' predicament, while accepting the fact that what was done was for the best.

If your child was older when he or she joined your family you may have a life story book about them. This will have been written at a particular point in time and will probably be a very general summary of what the child may have experienced. It is useful in going through this not just to read it but to check your child's understanding of what is written. Sometimes adoptive parents can be quite taken aback by young children's very blunt way of talking about problems like a parent's abuse of alcohol, but if your child is going to be able to deal with this, you must be too. This can also help you find out ways that the life story book needs to be added to in the future, both with the child's new experiences within your family and his or her growing understanding of their past.

If your child was freed for adoption when he or she joined you the application to adopt is likely to be fairly straightforward and the timing will be judged on your growing relationship and a recognition of your child's growing security with you. You may, of course, need to explain the details of the court process and the visit of the guardian *ad litem*, in Scotland the curator *ad litem*. However, other older children are placed under different legal provisions and the adoption order or petition may be actively contested. If your child is old enough to be aware of this, this is likely to be a very unsettling time for him or her as well as causing you anxiety. Of course your social worker and legal representative will be actively involved in supporting and guiding you.

Your child will also need to be able to discuss what is happening with you. In these situations it is usually best to make it clear that while their views and wishes are important and the court will want to hear about them, the decisions will be taken by the adults. Some children at such a time can feel very conflicting loyalties and need a lot of reassurance that they are not being asked to forget or reject their birth parents. Some can feel that they are being asked to make choices or that in order to convince everyone where they want to be, the adopters need to be all "good" and their birth parents "bad". This does not help in the longer term with a healthy integration of their two families: what part of their adult identity came from their birth family, their genetic inheritance and early experiences, and what part from their experiences of positive parenting in their adoptive family.

Adopters in these situations are now frequently given a great deal of background information to help them understand the basis for a contested case and decide if they can accept the degree of risk. This may also include information about full or half-brothers and sisters who are elsewhere. Clearly your child or children will need to know about these other family members, where they are and why they are not together. At the same time you will need to discuss carefully with your social worker the issue of sharing details of what happened to these other brothers or sisters – particularly if this includes other distressing events. There are always balances to be sought between helping your child understand his or her own circumstances and why certain decisions were made and not overwhelming children with a lot of difficult information that may not have directly involved them. Equally your child is likely to be helped by knowing that not only will you be honest with him or her, but also that you understand this is very sensitive personal information and that you respect each child's need for some privacy about their individual circumstances.

6

Helping your child to remember

Baby adopters often have very limited information and it's OK to go back to the agency and ask for more. Our son came to us when he was eight weeks old. We made a book about those first eight weeks (very slim!) but we had to ask the adoption agency for more to put into it. A social worker went off to the hospital where he was born, which was 200 miles away from us, and took a photo for us! We went back to the agency and were able to read more information in the file. It helped fatten the book a little more! Our photocopy of the birth certificate is the most treasured bit of it now that he's 16.

Children who remain with their birth families throughout childhood have many ways of knowing about their past. Their parents and relatives, including older brothers or sisters, have memories and stories to tell. During childhood some of these stories become part of the family history, to be brought up and laughed about or wondered over again and again. Often there are photograph albums or sometimes home made videos of the child at different stages of growing up. Most people know if they were born in hospital, at a nursing home or at home, and many know the time of birth and who was involved, for example, if a friend or relative helped look after any other children in the family at the time. As children grow up, other events like moving house, going to nursery school, accidents, illnesses, friendships and family celebrations like birthdays and weddings, all become part of the family folk-lore of shared experiences.

For children separated from their birth parents, it is different. They have no family "keepers of their personal history". They

> A significant event came when we were writing my daughter's life story. She wrote: 'I always thought it was my fault I was taken away,' something she had never voiced but felt able to write and subsequently to talk about. She was then able to accept that circumstances beyond her control, and beyond the control of her parents, had caused it all to happen. Harder things to face such as sexual abuse have also been best dealt with initially through the medium of the life story book leading to discussions on a personal level; the action of writing unpleasant things allowing a more detached way in. She has even said, 'Oh dear, I knew I would have to write this awful part one day'. But she has faced up to it and seems relieved to have done so. When I suggested that some day she might want to destroy the unpleasant parts of her book she said 'Oh no, I couldn't do that, it's part of my life'. So now when she wants to share her book with someone the difficult pages are temporarily removed and only left in for a handful of very trusted people.

have to rely on outsiders like social workers or staff at children's homes and hospitals, and medical records. For these children – like your adopted child – their past is often a mystery or a jumbled collection of memories that no one can ever precisely put into place.

Luckily, social workers and others involved have begun to realise that helping children understand and come to terms with what went on in their early lives is the best way to enable them to move forward into the present and future. Depending on the age of your child and the circumstances, you may already have a life

Cover stories

When your child makes new friends or meets new people (like teachers), they will ask questions. It is vital that your child has answers ready and does not start making things up which can be so difficult to put right later. Make sure that your child has an explanation ready for the things that may seem odd to an outsider. Being adopted is not something to be ashamed of, but it is something that needs explaining; unfortunately, the general public's view of adoption is often still very old-fashioned. One mother told us, 'My daughter came home from school upset. A child had told her that adoption means that her mum had given her away and had never loved her. She was very hurt and bewildered. She was anxious to hear again how she was adopted, that her mum had loved her so much and had wanted only the best for her but was worried that she could not provide this.' Help your child to be prepared for this kind of thing and to be ready with answers – answers which are the truth, if not the whole truth.

story book for your child. Sometimes these story books may give you information to talk about with your child about why they are separated from their parents and some details of what happened to them. They may not necessarily include all the day-to-day events, outings or special times shared with their birth parents.

If you have the chance to meet the birth parents, they might be able to fill in more about their memories and will appreciate your understanding and valuing such memories. If not, they or other members of the birth family may be able to contribute some details if approached. If you do not receive a life story book for your child, think about starting one, even if your child was only a few weeks old when he or she came to you.

Look through what you already have that could form part of your child's personal history book. Photographs, letters, cards and any other documents are a good start. But if your child joined

Our daughter, adopted when she was seven, shies away from asking personal questions or referring to her life before she joined our family, and very often we have to look for opportunities to refer to her first six years. Because this was a time when she did not have a normal family life, she is often too anxious to blot out and forget these years. In an effort to help her sort out her very muddled memories and to fill in the gaps, we started to make a book. It took a good deal of persistence to get any relevant information from the social services department, and eventually I sent the social worker a long list of questions saying I would be grateful if only a few of them could be answered. I knew it was possible for him to visit her biological mother as she had been contacted in order to sign the consent form. I included all sorts of questions in the hope of gleaning information about her early babyhood and, considering the passage of time, I was grateful for the answers I received.

We then started slowly over many months to build her life story book. As writing was then a considerable labour for her I did most of the simple factual writing leaving her to put in the important information such as the date of her birth, where she was born, her first name, etc. We were able to illustrate the book with pictures and maps of the place of her birth, and we were fortunate in being able to obtain some photographs through various social workers and house-parents. Working on the book has given us both a wonderful opportunity to deepen our relationship in discussing a very intimate part of herself.

Life story work

If you decide to make a life story book with your child, you could invest in another BAAF book which goes into the subject in much greater detail and offers much practical advice and guidance. *Life Story Work* by Tony Ryan and Rodger Walker includes lots of suggestions for clarifying your child's past – making maps of the local area with moves marked, playing with dolls and models to indicate family members, drawing up family trees and much more (see Useful Books). An example from the book is shown here.

you past babyhood, most of all you need to depend on your child's memory and on the contacts you have who can help you, in particular, workers at the adoption agency who placed your child with you. If you use a loose-leaf folder, it means you can add to it as more details emerge. It also enables the child to remove any particularly private bits before showing the book to friends or relatives, if they want to.

Remember that this may not be an easy exercise. Your child may not want to remember some of his or her early experiences, but to make a life story book all known facts should be included. You would be well advised to talk to the social worker who worked with your child before you start. Your child may get angry during the time you are working on the book and may take it out on you, the old hurt and bewilderment coming back. But you are undoubtedly the best person to do this work; you know your child better than anyone else does now, and you have the opportunities that no one else has. You can choose the times when your child is in the right mood to do this kind of thing. You can continue for as short or as long a time as you want. And, because you are now your child's family, you can do this task from a safe, secure base. You can use these times with your child for building on the warm loving relationship of the present. And as the book comes up to date, you can start adding the memories of the present to those of the past.

If you know that some parts of the life story book may be upsetting to your child, it is a wise precaution to make copies of photographs and important documents, especially letters. It is not unknown for life story books to be "lost" or destroyed. Of course, books are not the only means of keeping memories and some children may specially value having a safe place in which to keep items from the past – perhaps a toy or piece of clothing or gifts from birth family members.

7

If your child is of a different ethnic origin

Possibly the most vital thing of all is to try and stay in touch with our children, to talk with them, to learn from them. You may not face the frequent put-downs and slights, or worse, that they do, but you can share their humiliations and embarrassments, and discuss with them ways of dealing with racism – when to confront people or when to walk away with dignity. You can play your part too by refusing to watch unacceptable programmes on TV, and by openly expressing your disgust over racist comments and action expressed in the media or by people you meet. These skills can be made easier if you can ask black people to help you.

If your child is of a different ethnic origin from
you, then you have an additional responsibility and some extra
explaining to do. This chapter addresses issues of relevance to
white adoptive parents who have adopted a black child. By
'black' we mean a person who, as a result of his or her ethnicity,
is visibly different and will meet responses, including racism,
from others in the community as a result of this. It includes those
who have at least one parent who may be African, African-

What else can you do?

Every day, your child hears the word "black" used to
mean "wrong" and the word "white" to mean "right".
Think of "getting a black mark", "blacklisted", "in a black
mood", "blackmail", "black market", and so on. All these
terms have a negative meaning. Where does this leave
your black child? No wonder the phrase "black is
beautiful" was coined: black people need to believe in
themselves, just like everyone else does. At least in your
family and social circle, you can try to avoid using words
in this way. Try to put yourself in your child's place, and
be sensitive to their feelings. If you go on using "black"
to mean something bad, you too are helping to give your
child a poor impression of their colour and themselves.

Caribbean, Asian, Chinese, Arab or from another specific ethnic
group. It thus includes a considerable range of heritages and its
use is not intended to eliminate the need to take individual
heritage into account for each child and family.

You are likely to be aware that there has been a lot of discussion
around what are termed "transracial" placements, that is, where
white people have adopted a black child, and that there is a lot
of emphasis now on finding "same-race" placements for
children, that is, where black children are adopted by families
that share their ethnic background. This is a much wider subject
than we can address in this book but the important thing to

remember is that when children are adopted into a family, the priority for everyone should be making that the best possible experience for each child. You may feel uncomfortable about some aspects of this or want to debate it – open questioning of such issues is healthy.

Obviously children and families will have differing views and experiences, but over the years we have heard from many black children and young people who have been fostered or adopted. They, like many black children living within their birth families, have thoughts and feelings about what it is like to grow up in Britain and look identifiably different. In helping and supporting them, black parents draw on their own personal experiences, but for white parents, there is the added responsibility of finding out more about their child's reality. It is particularly painful to talk to young people who are completely confused, not being able to talk with their adoptive parents either about their

> I also remember trying to talk to people about my origins and would ask questions like, 'why am I black?', or 'where did my real father come from?'. The answers I would receive would be along the lines of, 'it's nothing to worry about, you are British' or 'England is your home, you are one of us'. These answers may well have been well-meaning, but when I was older I was bitter about them.
>
> My strong advice to white families offering homes to black children is to be honest with them when they want to talk about such sensitive issues. Don't be afraid to discuss with them their origins or the harsh realities of the world outside. If need be, get support from relations or friends or people from outside the immediate family rather than shy away from the subject. It may well be that such discussions will cause stress or hurt to your child at times, but warmth, love and honesty and really sharing sensitive issues will overcome stress or hurt. The benefits that will be given are that your child will grow and develop and will very likely be a more well adjusted person who is able to face the realities of what life can be like without the protection of the family.

adoption or their experience of being clearly of a different racial origin from both friends and family. Although it might seem that these adoptions must be more open as the child's difference is obvious, "visibility" is not, in itself, openness – this relies on the ability of the adults to enable the child to talk and communicate freely.

Where can you get more help?

You may like to encourage your child's school to use some excellent materials from the Afro-Caribbean Education Resource Project (ACER), Wyvil School, Wyvil Road, London SW8 2TJ. ACER has produced a series of books for younger children called *I'm special myself*: the set of four includes *Me*, *My Body*, *My Senses* and *My Feelings*.

Also useful are two little books for black children in a series called *Black like me*. The first one, *Black identity*, aims to encourage a positive self-image and the second, *Black pioneers*, describes the work of black inventors, scientists, doctors and civil rights campaigners. Available from the National Children's Bureau, 8 Wakley Street, London EC1V 7QE.

Like all adopted children, your child has already "lost" his or her birth parents: it's up to you to ensure that all that went with those parents is not lost too. Your child needs to know about these things. Of course, like all adopters you need as much information as you can get about your child's birth parents as described on earlier pages. But you need much more than this. In today's society, people from minority ethnic groups are often portrayed by newspapers and television in a very negative way, or marginalised, or ignored altogether, although this is slowly changing. But it is important to consider the following: How often does your child see black people featured in TV advertisements? How many characters in comics are black? How many books about black children are available for your child to read? The answer to all these questions is probably 'Not many'. And even when black people are portrayed in the media, it is often in stereotyped or negative ways, or show only limited facets of black people's experiences and achievements, for example, in connection with "inner city crime" or in sport. While this has

Thoughts on adoption

'I was brought up in a fairly multi-national family...We were all surrounded by love – unconditional, unprejudiced, unyielding, indiscriminatory love. My family, in many ways, is/was a real 'text book' success story. I was no different from my white brothers and sisters and I grew and became very confident from that nexus of love. Now, however, I feel my family's approach to loving me in the idyllic colour-blind way is, sadly, totally unrepresentative of society's acceptance of me as Anna. I am non-white living in a predominantly white racist society. As much as their love gave me strength, confidence and happiness (which is not to be marginalised), it also gave me a false sense of myself...I know that I have hurt people I love with this sudden awareness and subsequent anger. That is not my intention, but I am in a state of turmoil. This is a big voyage of self-discovery which, at times, is very painful. A lot remains unresolved as yet. I know I will work through this somehow – if only because I have the support and love of my adoptive family which is evident in so many ways. I need to be listened to and comforted if necessary, yet I also need them to encourage me on this journey and learn from my pain and not feel guilty or fractured by it, or try and appease me.'

This is taken from *Thoughts on Adoption* by black adults adopted as children by white parents. This is a short paper produced by the Post Adoption Centre in London and originates from a group run for transracially adopted adults called ATRAP (see Useful Organisations). It combines a general summary of the key factors emerging from the group with the personal views of three of the group members. Details about obtaining this, and another discussion paper, *A Glimpse through the Looking Glass*, which lists issues arising from an earlier group for transracially adopted black adults, can be found in Useful Books.

been recognised for some time, change is slow and patchy. Yet, as we know, the vast majority of black people in this country, just like the vast majority of white people, are law-abiding middle-of-the-road folk, going about their daily business in the same way as anyone else. So it is up to you to set the record straight. You have to challenge these stereotypes your child faces every day and in many subtle forms. So first of all it is vital that you have a positive attitude towards your child's ethnic background.

Direct contact with people who have similar ethnic origins to your child is obviously helpful. You may already have friends who can help you or have links with multicultural networks. Not only will you be able to find out much more about your child's heritage, but you will also be giving them a positive picture, that is, adults of their own heritage to look up to. The black child in a white family is not only in a minority in society but in their own family too. How much more important, then, is it for you to help your child in any way you can to cope with what the rest of society is presenting them with. To do this you need the support of black people who share the experience and so understand better than you do what your child has to face.

As well as the many subtle ways your child is told that black is less valuable than white, there is also open racism and children can face this from a very early age. Racial abuse is different from any other kind of insult. Imagine being called a "white bastard" or "whitey" as if the word "white" were an insult in itself – it's difficult, isn't it? Yet black children have grown used to this. Sooner or later your child will face racism and racist insults: will they come to you for help? Or will they see you on the same side as those who have insulted them because of your colour?

Colour cannot be ignored. At the earliest age, your child needs to be aware that there are people of different colours in the world and that no one colour is better than another. In previous pages we discussed the earliest stages of a child's introduction to adoption, and we recognised that important period when, although they have limited understanding of words and little or no understanding of concepts, they begin to perceive differences and attach values to them. From observations of small children in playgroups and nursery school, it is increasingly accepted that children are aware of different skin colour by about the age of two and at the ages of three and four are rating such characteristics as more or less desirable. At this early age, your child will also be becoming aware that he or she is a different colour from you. Your child will not have a real understanding of why, or the link with adoption, but the words to explain can be introduced and the open discussion of both different ethnic origins and adoption clearly established.

If you have built up a warm understanding relationship with your child based on open discussion about ethnicity and colour, and have included in your circle of friends people from other ethnic backgrounds, your child will recognise that although much of society may hold racist views, at least you do not. Your chances then of maintaining a good relationship with your child, and of supporting him or her when confronted with racism, right through the adolescent years and into adulthood, are that much better.

While adolescence can be a confusing and difficult period for many teenagers, it may be particularly turbulent for some young black people in white families. Sorting out their developing sexuality may be more complex when related to some of the stereotypes of black males and females. The normal adolescent phase of developing independence from the family can be stronger if linked to a desire to make contact with the black community and find an identity as a black adult. Part of this may be a need to seek out the black birth parent. Despite the potential struggles of this period, many black adopted teenagers maintain their strong attachment to their adoptive families and that relationship is more likely to be weakened if their adoptive parents have difficulty in accepting their emerging black identity.

If your child is from a different country

So the day of the court hearing came. I told Shanti afterwards that the nice man who had smiled at her (the judge!) had said that she could really and truly be our little girl forever. Of course she doesn't remember this but from then on, all we did was to answer all her questions as truthfully as we could. Often she would ask, 'Didn't my mother love me?' and I always said, 'Yes, she did. She couldn't keep you because there was no daddy and no money and she wanted you to have a daddy, a mummy and brothers and sisters.' (We have three older children born to us.) The first day she was at school, as she ran out calling, 'Mummy!' another child said, 'That's not your real Mummy!' My heart sank for her, but she said, 'Yes she is! She's not my first Mummy, but she's my real Mummy'. Now that was entirely her own choice of words.

Intercountry adoption is an area that has been the subject of a lot of discussion and controversy for a number of years. If you adopted your child a number of years ago you may have come across at least ambivalence, if not actual discouragement, from the authorities in the UK. Now, while the philosophical debates continue, most people embarking on an intercountry adoption will find a more consistent approach to the completion of a home study and more attention paid to preparation for the additional needs of these children. At the same time you may now find you are more comfortable joining in any local post-adoption support services.

Some intercountry adopters in the past have felt a sense of isolation on the outside of the normal "domestic" adoption service (see Chapter 23 of *After Adoption* in Useful Books). Earlier in this book we have mentioned the importance of the feelings of the adults and how these can affect the confidence of adoptive parents in talking to their children. Alongside the whole range of emotions experienced by any adopters, those who go down the intercountry route may, in addition, have a sense of disapproval which can lead to defensiveness – or perhaps a sense of personal achievement at surmounting many obstacles! You will need to think about whether this affects you and how you will answer any challenges about why you made the choice to adopt your child.

One of the factors that may affect you in this is the way intercountry adoption is covered in the media. As your child grows up, he or she is likely to become more aware of this. You will need to think about what could be triggered off for them.

Some television programmes and articles in newspapers focus on the overwhelming needs of children in other countries and for many adoptive parents the desire to help even one such child is a significant starting point.

Other programmes or articles may focus on investigating those who have made money out of exploiting both very poor parents in the developing countries and also the emotions of those desperate to become parents. With younger children you may be able to be selective about what they see in the media. Sometimes features in the press or on TV can be very helpful in opening up discussions with your child and laying the foundations for future talk about their intercountry adoption. If you're not sure, videoing a programme on TV in advance can help you prepare for likely questions.

With older children, they are more likely to find such programmes or articles themselves, especially if they are at an age of needing to know more about their adoption. Or they may pick up information from friends. You may need to talk directly to your child both about how you came together and also about the safeguards that are increasingly being built into intercountry adoption. If you went through all the official channels both here and in the country your child came from, this may be quite straightforward to explain. However, if you adopted some time ago, all the procedures that now exist both in the UK and in a growing number of "sending" countries may not have been in place. Of course much of what was included in, for example, the 1993 Hague Convention on the Protection of Children and Co-operation in Respect of Intercountry Adoption was based on experience built up over many years. Regardless of the particular structures that existed when you adopted, there may be a lot you can say about your time in your child's country of origin that reflects your respect for and understanding of their birth parents' predicament. At the same time the reality is that you may have no specific information about your child's birth parents or the pressures they were under. You may only be able to express your sorrow about the way things were and say that you hope their birth family would be pleased about their child's present life.

Of course many people consider intercountry adoption after first

of all undergoing prolonged fertility investigations and then
exploring adoption in the UK only to discover how few babies are
placed for adoption now. As you will already know, intercountry
adoption is not an easy road and, as your child grows older, he or
she may become very aware of your strong desire to become an
adoptive parent and all the effort involved in adopting them.
Particularly during adolescence they may have many questions
about how you balanced your own need to parent with the needs
of both themselves and their birth parents. (See *Why Adoption* by
Kulwinder Sparks which includes a questionnaire put together by
an adopted teenager which, amongst other questions, asks why
her own and some other adoptive parents took that step).

The other question that comes up strongly for many children
adopted through the intercountry route is about being "rescued"
and if people think they should be grateful. 'Descriptions of the
conditions for many people in a number of countries, and
photographs of life in many "orphanages" underline this.
This, however, in the long term isn't comfortable for a child.

Generally of course new adoptive parents, while being aware of
the conditions in which "their" child has been living, quickly
become involved in a growing relationship with this new little
person. All the personal descriptions of this early stage soon push
thoughts of "rescue" aside as all the parent–child emotions take
over. If you already have birth children in your family, they too
may be eager to help you offer care to this child who has suffered
adverse circumstances. Initially they may need your guidance on
finding the balance between the extra attention the incoming
child might need and the importance of helping him or her
become an "ordinary" family member.

You may need to think about possible comments from people
outside the family or strangers. The fact that your child may look
very different from you may cause comment to which you will
need to find a response. When your child is young there may be
comments in front of him or her along the lines of, 'Isn't it

wonderful to have done that' and later the child may be told he
or she is "lucky". A ready response indicating you think the child
has brought at least as much into your life, if not a lot more,
than you've given to him or her can help your child make their
own response later. You may be able to suggest replies to them
like, 'Well, my mum and dad say they think they're lucky to have
me too – so I think we *all* like being part of our family'.

Your child's ethnic identity

A small number of the intercountry adoptions in
the UK involve either the adoption of a related child who has
been living in another country or families living here from a
minority ethnic group adopting from their country of origin. The
majority, however, involve British families adopting children of a
different cultural heritage. Very many of the children are also of
a different ethnic origin and the issues identified for transracial
adoptions of black and minority ethnic children equally apply.

However, some of the comments made to transracially adopted
children might have deeper meanings or different connotations
for those who arrived in their family through intercountry
adoption. For example, the question, 'So where are you from?'
which can carry hidden messages might feel different depending
on whether it is asked of a black child born in this country or
someone brought here from another country (see Chapter 22 in
After Adoption). A simple 'I was born in … but I live here now'
may deal with curiosity but you may need to help your child
think of replies they can make without having to reveal private
information they would prefer to keep personal. Sometimes it is
enough to say, 'Why do you ask?'

However, as he or she gets older your child may also need advice
about what to do if questions go beyond curiosity and become
nearer to bullying.

Like any other adoptive parent you will want to know as much as

possible about your child's origins to help them as they grow up.
Often, however, you might have very little information about
your child's birth parents and limited opportunity to find out
more. Those adopters who have vivid memories of meetings with
birth family members value the opportunities they had for
gaining a real understanding of the birth mother's circumstances, and photographic records of such events can underline
the mother's support of the adoption as the best prospect for
her child.

However, for many families your child's personal life story book
may have to start with your arrival in their life. Much of the
background information may focus on your child's country of
origin and cultural heritage rather than individual family details.
Just as earlier parts of this book emphasised the importance of
showing your sympathy and understanding for your child's birth
parents, so it is important to give a rounded picture of your
child's country of origin. It is not always easy to present your
child's country of origin in a positive manner when one of your
reasons for adoption may have been a wish to give them a better
life away from there. Probably the most straightforward starting
point is gathering together information about the history,
geography, religion and culture of your child's country of origin.

In the summer 1987 edition of *Adoption UK*, the PPIAS
newsletter, Roger Fenton provided a list of over 20 different
ways of obtaining such information, from use of public libraries,
pen friends, international exhibitions through to ideas for
sending a child to school for a period in their own country of
origin, perhaps through an exchange. If this was done now, the
Internet would be likely to feature prominently with the growing
array of information shared by others who have adopted from
abroad. Exploring all this information as a family can be very
pleasurable for both parents and children. Often nursery schools
and school teachers are happy to incorporate knowledge of
different cultures through projects. At the same time your child
may not always appreciate being picked out as being different or

coming from some "exotic" country that they may not remember much about.

The social and political history of the country your child comes from may be more complex to share. Adopted adults here in learning of their own origins and background elsewhere, also need to learn of the different social climate perhaps 30 or 40 years ago. This can help them to understand why their mother placed them for adoption when they appreciate just how difficult it used to be for single young women to keep their babies. Their adoptive parents will, of course, have been very aware of that. Adopting now from other countries, however, you may not necessarily have the same real understanding of what it is like living within a very different culture. Much of what we see on television or read about is from a very Western perspective and viewed through our eyes from the outside. Many intercountry adopters have very vivid memories of their time in their child's country of origin, though inevitably these are focused around meeting their child. A real "feel" for the people of a country and the influences that have shaped their current situation provides a lot of food for thought. This needs to underpin efforts to help your child understand his or her transcultural and/or transracial identity, particularly during adolescence.

A small number of intercountry adoptions are of older children. For example, upheavals over the last few years in Eastern Europe plus events like the disaster in Chernobyl have led to a growth in different forms of aid to a number of countries. In

Ji Sun was born in Korea and brought up in Belgium where she was adopted by her Swiss mother and Swedish father. This is a quote from an article, "A ghost in my country", written in 1996, after visiting Korea for the first time, aged 26.

'I felt the Westernised mask peeling off and fleetingly experienced a feeling of belonging, but I was living in limbo, unable to understand those who looked like me, unnoticed by Westerners whom I could not understand.'

some instances people who have not started off seeking an intercountry adoption had ended up doing so. In bringing aid to orphanages in Eastern European countries individual workers have formed an attachment to a particular child. In other instances, children may have come to Britain temporarily for medical attention and it may subsequently have seemed in their best interest to remain here. The child's wishes and feelings will be important in such cases and, as with older children adopted within the UK, they will already be well aware of their situation and probably will have considerable experience of their cultural heritage. Prospective adopters in this situation may have built an ongoing link with the child's country and may also have contact with other family members about the adoption. Medical, educational and social opportunities gained by the adoption may be apparent. What needs to be considered is the understanding of the life-long implications of adoption and the effect of the legal transfer of parental responsibilities.

One point which may be significant to some adopted people is what the effect of the adoption is on their status within their own country. The extent to which a country "closes the door" on a child who has been adopted into another country can have both practical and emotional implications for the future. If records are not kept (as they are in the UK) for 70 years, tracing in the future may be very difficult if not impossible. It may also not be possible for children to retain citizenship of their own country. Some adopted people need to return to their country of origin as adults. The can be very emotional and can be emphasised if their country does not acknowledge their existence.

If your child has a disability

I wrote down a little story for my daughter which I called 'Emma is adopted'. It's very easy, with a sentence or two on each page, and photographs of her and us. It tells the story of how she came to us in a very simple way, with lots of repeated bits. She's always loved it. At one time we used to have to read it to her half a dozen times a day. Now she's taken it all in, but she still goes back to it sometimes and we build on it and add pages. I can't think of a better way.

If you have adopted a child with a physical disability, your task will not be different from that of other adopters. Of course your child still has a right to know about his or her origins, just as any child does, and of course the dangers of your child finding out about their adoption accidentally are just as serious as for any adopted child. Indeed, because your child probably feels "different" already, finding out that they are different in yet another way – by being adopted – could be particularly devastating. Not only have they a disability, they may also feel that they have been rejected by their birth parents because of it. But you have an extra strength to offer your child: you really did choose him or her, disability and all. And, in a world where disability usually means "disadvantage", this is very important. Telling your child that he or she was chosen because of, and not in spite of, their disability may make up for some of their feelings of difference.

Your child's birth parents, too, may be different from others whose children are adopted; they may be a securely settled married couple with other able-bodied children. The explanations you give your child, therefore, have to stress the positive side of their placement with you. Whatever their situation at the time, the birth parents probably gave up their child because they wanted the best for him or her. You, the adopters, were able to offer this "best": perhaps you had much more experience of looking after a person with a disability, or have access to specialised facilities, or live near a particular hospital or school, or your family lifestyle could readily include and welcome a child with a specific impairment. Whatever the reason, you are the best family for your child.

For some children, their disability may bring up additional questions that you may need to tackle as your child grows older. Your child may have a genetically determined condition and need counselling on this aspect. Some adoptive parents find that while they gain a lot from joining self-help groups for parents of

children with a particular disability, when it comes to feelings
aroused by genetic issues, they are at a loss. If you are in this
position, you may need to go back to the agency which arranged
the adoption to ask if there is any further medical information
that could be shared, especially as medical knowledge advances.

A particular challenge faced by the adoptive parents of a few
children is the fact that their child's disability was caused by
their birth parent(s). There is, of course, no easy answer here
and inevitably hearing what has happened to some children and
seeing the permanent damage caused creates a range of angry

Who is my real mummy?

It might help, if your child asks questions like: 'But who is
my real mummy?', to in turn ask simple questions like:
Who puts you to bed? Who takes you to school? Who
reads you stories? Who do you feel is your real mummy?
Who do you want when you wake up in the night? Of
course, you want them to understand about their birth
mother too; if you approach it gently, you'll probably
find that your child can cope with the idea of two
mothers, both real in different ways.

and distressed feelings. It is essential to talk these feelings over
thoroughly with your partner, or in a support group, or to a
professional counsellor, so that, in the long run, they do not get
in the way of working out what would be most helpful to tell
your child about his or her origins and life history. It might also
be helpful to try networks like the PPIAS Resource Bank (see
Useful Organisations) to see if you can find other families who
have already met the same problems.

If your child has a learning disability

The fact that your child has a learning disability does not mean
he or she loses the right to know about and understand his or

her own life story. Indeed, the distress and confusion your child could feel on finding out about his or her adoption unexpectedly could, because of a more limited understanding, make this an even more threatening experience than usual. So you will need to find ways of explaining things at your child's own level. It will probably take longer for these children to understand each point, so it needs a much slower, gentler pacing with a lot more repetition. As their parent, you will know best when they are ready to take in simplified stories about their past, and how long it will take them to comprehend each new idea. And just as you are developing their potential in other ways, so you can help them to understand their early experiences too. If you feel that you need expert advice in this difficult field, contact one of the organisations listed in Useful Organisations.

Already in this book we have looked at what we now know about children's understanding of adoption and how we can see parallels with their sexual development and their learning in this area. So too with children with learning disabilities; we need to look for ideas to help these children develop their knowledge and understanding of themselves, their bodies, and their sexuality.

However profound your child's disability, and however limited

> **One area of potential difficulty with a severely disabled child like David is finding ways to help him build a positive self-image. As he struggles against frustration and a growing awareness of his difficulties and limitations, emphasis needs to be placed on those aspects of his life that he can develop and control, for example, personal relationships, intellectual skills, social contact. An adopted or fostered child may also have to cope with the knowledge that he has already been rejected because of his disabilities and David often seeks reassurance that I knew he couldn't walk and still wanted him. It is painful to answer his many questions about why he can't walk or write or draw, but I have always answered truthfully but simply, and it does seem to help him to verbalise his feelings about his disabilities.**

their understanding may seem, it's still worth going through the explaining process with them. At some level they will grasp that now they have consistent loving care from the same person or people, and that's the most valuable message to convey.

| Your child's story

Stories are always a good way of telling young children new things. In the section titled Useful Books we have listed some basic illustrated books you might find helpful in explaining things to your child. You will need to think about which books your child will accept. Some older children may only be able to manage a very simple text but would be put off by "babyish" pictures. Some of the commercially produced books about adoption may be suitable, but you will need to judge if your child can make the connections. Some children are confused by stories about other children, or animal stories, and need something that is very clearly and precisely about themselves.

Just like any other child, your child is likely to be fascinated by a story about himself or herself. All the details about being a baby, leaving the hospital, and the gradual process of growing up, illustrated with photographs and documents, will delight most children. Of course you will have to move at your child's pace, but all parents have to do this. And you will probably have to repeat the same points over and over again, but this too is very common. You may have to work hard to make them realise the "story" is about them, but it will be worth it. Some parents have found that a tape of the child's own story, which they can listen to repeatedly, is a very useful way of explaining. You will know best how simple to keep your child's story, because you know your child best. You will also know about the concrete actions that will confirm what you are saying to your child. Some children with disabilities find computers help them to communicate; multimedia computers may help these children to develop their own lifestory.

10

If you are a step-parent or other relative

We thought adopting the children would make us into a 'real' family and Colin would be much more their father than before. But actually it caused some problems. The kids didn't want him to order them about, and he felt that with the added responsibility, he could. It took ages before they accepted him and even now there are some arguments about it.

If you are a step-parent who has adopted, or who is thinking of adopting, your step-children, most of what appears elsewhere in this book will also be relevant to you and your step-children. Stepfamilies are on the increase, but adoption by step-parents has decreased. Because currently adoption cuts off legal ties with one birth parent, other arrangements are now seen as more appropriate, particularly where the child has strong links with the absent parent (who we've called the "other birth parent" in this section).

Many step-parents have adopted their step-children and in some cases, where the children were young enough not to realise, have kept this information from the child. But in England and Wales when a step-parent adopts, the parent with custody (the step-parent's husband or wife) has to become an adopter as well because it must be a joint application; usually this means the mother and the stepfather together adopting the child. The child therefore has an adoption certificate. This was the position in Scotland too until 1996. Now because of a change brought in by the Children (Scotland) Act 1995, a step-parent can adopt their wife's or husband's child without the birth parent becoming a joint adopter. But again this information would be shown on the child's new birth certificate. And at the age of 16 (in Scotland) or 18 (in England and Wales), the child can see the original birth certificate. Therefore the child will either have a current birth certificate showing both parents as adoptive parents with access

> Explaining it all to the children was the difficult bit... that they'd still be loved by their father and they should still love him, and he'd still be their father. The fact that I'd be married to someone else didn't mean that they couldn't still see him. Then there were all the questions about what to call my second husband – and who to make cards for on Father's Day. We got round that one by getting them to make two each, and I think they ended up being quite proud of the fact – it put them one up on the others in their class.

in the future to an original certificate with one of those adoptive parents named as birth parent, with or without the other biological parent. Or in Scotland they may have a current birth certificate with one birth parent and one adoptive parent again with subsequent access to the original certificate.

In thinking ahead to talking about this it might be helpful to keep a copy of the original birth certificate safely.

Adopting pre-school stepchildren

A situation that often arises is when a single mother subsequently marries a man who is not the father of the child and they wish to confirm that family unit, particularly where the stepfather is the only "father" the child has known. The legal process of adoption is often already started when the question of telling the child is brought up, and for people who have not been prepared for that, it is a good time to begin.

If you're thinking about adoption

BAAF has produced two leaflets about step-parents and adoption, one for England and Wales, and one for Scotland. These spell out the advantages and disadvantages of adopting for step-parents and tell you where to get more information. They are available from BAAF (see Useful Books).

There are not the same commercially produced simple story books for children in this situation but BAAF plans to publish an illustrated book for children that tells the story of a girl adopted by her stepfather (see Useful Books). Many families have also found it helpful to make their own story books with photographs. It is useful to sort out at this stage any areas that might be awkward to discuss as these may be different from other adoptions. For example, the child's parent (usually the mother) may still have very personal feelings about the absent birth parent – she may be angry or feel let down or feel embarrassed about talking about a relationship that she may regret or have pushed into the past. However, at this early stage, one or two simple facts, like the father's name, are all that is needed to help establish the truth and get over the initial hurdle in a gentle way. Fuller explanations can come later and you have time to sort out wording with which you are comfortable. Sometimes the step-parent fears that somehow he is in a secondary position as parent to this child and thought can be given to positive wording that emphasises that in marrying the birth mother he chose not only his partner but also freely embraced her child and made a commitment to both. This can be particularly useful as a focus if the "telling" has been left to a later stage when the step-parent may have concerns about the knowledge undermining a valued and well-established relationship with the child.

Adopting older children

For older children, where secrecy is not a possibility, other problems may appear. In cases of divorce, for example, the child may deeply resent the loss of the other birth parent. After all, divorce was not the child's idea and neither was the step-parent. The special relationship a child often has with a single parent is also put at risk by a step-parent. And children may worry that if they start to love their new step-parent, they'll somehow risk losing their other birth parent's love. The National Stepfamily Association can provide both information and support (see Useful Organisations).

These issues, which arise in many stepfamilies, can seem to be

> I was nine when my parents divorced and mum remarried when I was 11. At first I got on really well with my step-father and wanted him to adopt me, because we lost touch with my real father really quickly. But when I was a teenager it was nothing but rows over everything I did. Then I wished he hadn't adopted me! But we're OK now.

made more significant by adoption. It may make the child seem
more secure, or it may increase feelings of loss about the other
birth parent. Whatever the situation the child needs to be
consulted and listened to. If they are 12 or over in Scotland they
will be asked to sign their agreement to their adoption. Other
children need to be aware that their wishes will be taken into
account. Sometimes adults reach decisions that do not
completely accord with the child's wishes and they will need to
be helped to understand the reasons for this. It hurts when it
feels like you're losing a parent and equally it can be confusing
to some to think they have three parents. Of course, not all

What is a parent?

To help a child understand, it might be useful to explain
something about what being a parent means.

First and foremost, it means giving you life (your genetic
inheritance) and includes
the way you look
the way your brain and body work
some of the things you are good at and like to do
some of the things you find difficult and don't like

Secondly, it means caring for you and bringing you up:
loving you and minding what happens to you
encouraging you and comforting you
looking after you physically
teaching you all the things you need to know until you're
independent

Thirdly, it means taking responsibility for you:
making important decisions about things like schooling
and future plans
providing for you in material ways
representing your needs until you're old enough to do
this yourself

A child needs all these things, and for most children, they
all come from the birth parents. But for adopted children,
including those adopted by step-parents, where the birth
parent(s) aren't in a position to take on the second and
third areas, it means having two sets of parents.

children adopted by their stepfathers ever knew their birth fathers. But where the birth father is known, especially if he still keeps in contact with the child, it's up to you to make things clear. Life story books, as described earlier in Chapter 6, can work wonders here, with family trees showing where everyone fits in. And some of the children's books listed in Useful Books may also come in useful in the explaining process. It's hard work, but so are most relationships that are worth having.

Other adoptive situations

Some children are adopted by members of their extended family, like grandparents or aunts. In the past this was often in order to hide an illegitimate pregnancy and was shrouded in secrecy. For adopted adults this has led to special complications, not only about the shock of discovering their adoption but also because family secrets can create all sorts of tensions, particularly when you do not know how much different family members know or what thoughts and memories they might have of earlier events. While over the years this situation has changed, and many families are much more open in responding to the difficulties of individual members, sometimes such adoptions happen in the hope of providing security for a particular child. There is, for example, a clear difference between children knowing that they were adopted by their grandparents, and grandparents adopting a grandchild but bringing this child up as though they are the child's parents, which obviously complicates all other family relationships.

It is easy enough to say the same principles apply to any adoption, namely that children need to know and understand

> We decided to adopt Rachel when she was 7. She knew we were her grandparents and who her mum was – but she wanted to be the same as everyone else at school. She called us 'mum and dad' but she wanted to see us treated like that by people like her teachers. Fortunately our daughter agreed it was best too.

their origins, and that this is based on a gradually growing awareness linked to children's ability to understand at different stages of development; for such in-family adoptions there are some additional distinctive features. Firstly, it is not so much about the child integrating the knowledge of two families – the birth and the adoptive family – but rather about feeling confident of his or her position within the whole extended family. However, this may still only be the extended family of one parent, and the absent birth parent may be more firmly excluded while still being part of the child's origins. Secondly, when grandparents talk with the child about his or her birth parents, they are also discussing their own son or daughter and this can be upsetting, particularly if that son or daughter has been involved in a very problematic lifestyle like alcohol or drug abuse. If you are in this position you may need to call upon the support of other trusted family members or one of the adoption counselling services. Similar issues arise from talking with children about their origins and intimate family matters in many circumstances, not just in relation to "traditional" adoption (see post-adoption centres in Useful Organisations).

Reproduction assisted by new techniques of fertility treatment may now be another topic which is difficult to broach with children and which needs careful planning. As an example of 'finding the right words' a book called *My Story* which is aimed at children about four or five years old gives a simple explanation of donor insemination (see Useful Books). One particular response to infertility that directly leads to adoption is that of surrogacy. As in step-parent adoption, this can have different implications for two parents as the child may be genetically linked to the father but not the mother although adopted by both. As surrogate mothers usually have other children there is also the question of talking about their biological half-siblings as well as finding the right words to talk about why their birth mother would agree to have a baby that she would give away.

How adopted children feel

Whenever my parents told me off or wanted me to do something I didn't want to do, I'd say 'My real mum would have let me' or 'She'd have understood'. I didn't mean it ... I'd no idea whether she would or not, but it was a way of getting back at them. Somehow they put up with me even when I was trying to be so awkward like this. I even ran away twice but I went back. Later, when I met my first mother, I felt I had much more in common with them than with her after all. I didn't realise till years later how much this must have hurt them.

Of course every child's experience of adoption is personal and unique. Below are just a few brief examples of children's and young people's perceptions of their adoption. There are a number of books and specialist magazines that include further experiences of being adopted (see Useful Books).

When I first came to this family I was very frightened because I had been moved from different homes before – they had been horrid. So I thought that because the other homes were not very nice to me that this family was going to be horrid. The first night I came I was not used to so many people around the house and I was very confused, but soon – after about four weeks – I got used to my surroundings. Sometimes when social workers came I ran away into my bedroom because I thought that each time I would be taken away. I used to always think about the past. But my foster parents taught me to look into the future and what I would do and not what I had done.

I like living with my mummy and daddy and little sister. I grew in Maureen's tummy. I went to hospital to be born but then I had to live with somebody else. I was very sad but I loved my new parents. They loved me. I was adopted by my mummy and daddy. We went to court to see if I could live with them. The judge said yes. I grew up to be a big girl and now I am six. I wanted a little sister so mummy and daddy said I could. Once again we went to court to see if my little sister could live with us. The judge said yes. My sister is two now and I like playing with her.

I can think back to situations when, as a child, people were trying to protect me from some harsh realities that I had to face eventually as an adult anyway. If these people had been less protective and willing to talk, I think that I might have been better able to deal with some of the stressful situations I had to face as a young adult. When I had problems with people, and I honestly knew that those problems arose because I was black, people looking after me would say, 'Just ignore them, they are only ignorant and don't know you,' rather than helping me to cope by talking such issues through with me in order to help me understand better.

The fact that I was not born to my parents has never ever worried or saddened me; with loving and caring parents as I am lucky enough to have, whether or not we are related by blood does not matter to any of us. I feel that my sister and I belong as much to our parents as any of my friends do to their natural parents. My reaction, when asked what I feel about my other family in another country is that I don't have another family; I've only ever known one mother, one father and one sister. We are all able to talk very freely about my sister's and my first families but they seem so distant, hardly connected with us at all. It seems slightly unreal to me. Maybe I should feel closer to my first parents. I don't know. After all, it was thanks to them that I am part of a very close family now. I hope they don't miss me; I hope they are able to speak about me as I am able to speak about them. Although I was born to them and I knew them for nine months I feel it's not so much who you're born to, it's who you spend your life with that matters.

I wanted to be adopted when I understood what it meant. I did so want to be part of a family and stay for good. I began to get very ill because I wanted to be adopted. When I was adopted I cried with happiness. Now I have been adopted I feel safe. I can stay with my family for as long as I please and that will be for as long as I live. I love my family very much.

How birth parents feel

I'm a mother who had a child nearly twenty years ago, alone. The baby's father was not married and he could have married me if he had wanted to. I loved the father and I loved the baby all through the pregnancy and I loved her enough to give her away so that she could have a family. I would not have considered adoption if I had not thought that the adoptive parents had a lot more to offer than I could. My cherished wish is to meet them and to know how she is getting on.

As has been pointed out already in this book, it's important to try and understand your child's birth parents so that you can help him or her with knowledge about them. It's often difficult not to judge people but you may not know all the circumstances. As you can imagine, mothers (and fathers) who give up their children do not, by and large, do it easily! There is usually a lot of heartache and emotional turmoil involved. If your child came to you as a baby, you may like to read about some of the experiences of young mothers (see *Half a Million Women* and *Within me, Without me* in Useful Books). If your child was older, as is increasingly the case these days, think of the circumstances and try to put yourself in the birth parent's place. Remember that they will certainly feel a deep sense of regret and guilt at having 'lost' their child. Almost always, if they agreed to the adoption it was because they believed that it was the best for their child and was the most responsible thing they could do in the circumstances.

If the birth parents of your child did not agree to the adoption they may be left with a whole mixture of confused feelings. Mixed in with anger or guilt, there may be a tremendous sense of loss of a child of whom they have strong memories as they had lived together for a considerable period (see *Still Screaming* in Useful Books). Yet often these birth parents not only have extra problems in many areas of their lives, but have also cut themselves off from either family or professional support or find it hard to use or accept.

> **When I finally decided that the best thing for the kids was not to go on trying to bring them up myself, I felt very guilty at first. People didn't want to know me. But the ups and downs of me going in and out of hospital had really messed their lives up and I wanted them to have some stability. I know now that I was right, and not everybody else. Though I've missed them, they've had a much better chance than they would have had with me, as things turned out. I still think of them a lot, especially at Christmas and birthdays.**

As the years go by, if there is no contact between the birth
parents and the adopted child, many birth parents feel an
overwhelming sense of loss, particularly around the date of the

Can I trace my child?

As the law stands at present in Britain, adopted children
can see their birth certificates at 16 in Scotland or 18 in
England and Wales and this gives them the opportunity
to try to trace their birth parents. But there is no similar
legal right for birth parents who want to trace their
children. There are, however, ways in which birth parents
can record whether or not they would wish to be
contacted if their adoptive child is searching for them and
can provide up-to-date information to make this easier.
This can be done via the Adoption Contact Register
(England & Wales) and the Birthlink Register (Scotland)
(see Chapter 13).

Birth parents may also record such information on the
files held by the agency which placed their child.
Adoption files must be kept for 75 years and many
adoption agencies are making better provision for adding
extra information after adoption. The growing number of
Post or After Adoption services offer support to birth
parents too (see Useful Organisations). It may help for
birth parents to talk to counsellors or other birth parents.
As the needs of birth parents are more fully understood,
an increasing number of specialist workers are willing to
consider sensitive ways in which to let adoptive parents
and adopted people know that the birth parent has been
in touch and would welcome information about the
child's progress (see Chapter 13).

BAAF has produced a leaflet, *Child from the Past*, with
information for parents who placed a child for adoption
years ago in England and Wales. NORCAP (the National
Organisation for Counselling Adoptees and their Parents)
is also a useful source of information (see Useful
Organisations).

child's birth. As the time of the sixteenth or eighteenth birthday
approaches, many anticipate the phone call or letter that means

their child wants to make contact. If nothing happens they are kept in a state of uncertainty which is never far from the surface, though it may last years or even a lifetime.

Some parents, of course, feel differently. They may be in the position of having married and had other children and may never even have admitted to their partner that there was a previous child. They may feel dread at the thought of the "knock on the door". Just as openness about adoption is the best thing, so openness about one's past is often the only way to real peace of mind in these circumstances.

Explaining adoption to the birth parent's children

Many mothers whose children have been adopted in the past go on to have other children. They then have to decide whether or not to tell these children about their earlier child. In this situation, as in the others described in this book, honesty is usually the best policy. Whether or not these children have the right to know that they have another brother or sister is an

> **Adopted children often don't seek out their birth parents as they feel they were given away or not wanted. This is far from the truth. I was 18, naive, and vulnerable. I stayed at the mother and baby home until the birth of my daughter. We had choices but looking back I was manipulated into giving up my child: 'Surely, if you love your daughter, you want the best for her – two loving parents who can give her a good and secure home, etc.' So I was made to feel I had to give her up, love my baby as I did! But in all the time before the birth of my child and after not one person said to me, 'Have you thought of keeping your child?' Now, married with three further children, when each was born (and many more times besides) I have cried for the baby I should have kept. So my message to adopted people is: don't feel you were given up or unwanted. I wasn't the only young girl at the home and the majority were in the same boat.**

interesting question. But if the adopted child decides to look for his or her birth family, he or she and the rest of the family are likely to find out about it anyway. However, mothers in this position often find it very difficult to tell their children. They may worry that the children would be afraid of being given up too (depending on their age), or how it would make them appear – callous, hard-hearted, promiscuous perhaps. It can be very difficult for young people today, growing up surrounded by single parent families, to understand how different the world once was and what a stigma was attached to "illegitimacy". Nonetheless, the truth is still the best answer, with whatever detail the child can cope with at their age.

For other birth parents now, their family circumstances may be much more complex as are the reasons surrounding their child's adoption. This may include full or half brothers and sisters still at home with them or in other forms of care. While you may be struggling to find the right words to talk to your adopted child, the birth parents may be struggling even more to talk to other children or members of their extended family, especially while they may be feeling very bad about themselves and how they have coped with their lives, with their self esteem and confidence at a very low point.

My thoughts for my daughter's adoptive parents have always been kind. I hope that I will meet them. I know it's a lot to ask, but hopefully as our society is changing, they will not see me as a threat. I can understand their attachment, the pride and love they have shared. The extra love I have cannot hurt. Even if the only mistake I made was having her adopted, I have had to accept so many things concerning her. I hope that they will accept that I exist and that I love her, and that I also love her enough not to try and tear her away from a family that has brought her up and still loves her.

13

Tracing birth parents

I was adopted in 1930 and felt there was little chance of tracing my family as so many records were destroyed during the war. I thought I would be content to just have my original birth certificate but after my counselling session, I became really interested in my birth family and decided to search. The experience of searching has taught me a lot. Firstly, I didn't think I would become emotionally involved: I didn't think I was the type. I found there were days when I was elated and had to play music really loudly to let off steam. Other days I had to work extra hard to hide bitter disappointment. I felt I didn't want to talk about it. Patience was also essential, and being an impatient person, there were times when I was tempted to phone on the spur of the moment, and I'm ashamed to think of the distress this might have caused!

When they reach a certain age, adopted children in Britain have the right to see their original birth certificate. This means that they can find out the name of their birth mother, and sometimes father, if they do not already know it. They can also see the address their mother gave at that time. With this information they can, if they choose, try to trace their birth parent(s) and perhaps make contact with them. Not all adopted children do, and certainly not all at the age of 16 or 18 do, but the numbers are growing.

In Scotland it was always possible for adopted people to have access to their original birth certificate from the age of 17 (now 16) and so birth parents and adoptive parents should have been made aware of this at the time the adoption plan was being made. In England and Wales the right of adopted people from the age of 18 to see their original birth certificate was only introduced in 1976, so of course there are many birth parents who gave up their child for adoption before that time expecting never to have any future contact with them. Because of this, children who were adopted before that law came into force have to have an interview with a counsellor (usually a social worker) before they can see their birth certificate. This helps to give them a chance to think about the possible consequences for themselves and their birth parents if they wish to seek more information and actually consider tracing that birth parent. Children adopted more recently are not required to see a counsellor before getting their birth records. However, the effects of this step can be far-reaching and very emotional so that talking it over with a counsellor or objective outsider is strongly recommended.

The Children Act 1989 included provision for the Registrar General to set up the Adoption Contact Register for England and Wales. The Register is in two parts – Part I is a list of adopted people who have chosen to register and Part II a similar list of birth parents and other relatives of an adopted person. The

Register provides a safe and confidential way for birth parents
and other relatives to assure an adopted person that contact

> **The Adoption Contact Register and Birthlink**
>
> The purpose of the Adoption Contact Register in England
> and Wales is to put adopted people and their parents or
> other relatives in touch with each other *where this is
> what they both want.* The Register provides a safe and
> confidential way for birth parents and other relatives to
> assure an adopted person that contact would be welcome
> and to give a current address. A leaflet giving more
> information can be obtained from:
>
> Office for National Statistics (ONS, formerly OPCS), The
> General Register Office (England and Wales), Adoptions
> Section, Smedley Hydro, Trafalgar Road, Birkdale,
> Southport, Merseyside PR8 2HH. You will require to
> complete an application form and there is a fee for
> registration.
>
> Birthlink is Scotland's adoption contact register. It is
> confidential and it is a central point of contact for all
> those involved in the adoption process. Based in a
> voluntary social work charity, Birthlink is a free source of
> information though there may be a charge for some of
> the more in-depth services. Further information can be
> obtained from:
>
> Birthlink, Family Care, 21 Castle Street, Edinburgh
> EH2 3DN. Tel. 0131 225 6441

would be welcome and to give a current address; a leaflet giving
full details is available from them (see box). In Scotland a similar
adoption contact register called Birthlink has been available for a
number of years based in a voluntary adoption agency (see box).

Seeking information and making contact

Very many adopted adults now seek further information about
their birth parents or go on to make contact. Whether or not they

are required to seek counselling, a growing number do seek
support through what can be a very emotional period and there
is more and more knowledge and experience around now about
what can be involved (see *I'm Here Waiting* in Useful Books).
Some do not wish to go further than filling in some gaps in
background information, others may seek only limited contact
via an intermediary, and yet other people go on to seek direct
contact and are involved in reunions. These can initially be
highly charged emotionally and may or may not approach
anywhere near the hopes or expectations of the individuals
concerned. It can be useful to have relatively up-to-date
information about birth parents so as to be as realistic as
possible about their circumstances. However, some adopted
people have an overwhelming need to try and make contact at
certain points in their lives and may need a lot of support if it
does not work out as it was hoped. To find out more about the
whole range of experiences of reunions, you could contact
NORCAP (see Useful Organisations) which produces a regular
newsletter and there are some helpful books listed in Useful
Books.

Although they may want to explore these options for themselves,
some adopted adults are also very concerned about the impact of
that wish on their adoptive parents. Some hold back on their

> **I have reached the point where I absolutely must know
> the truth about my origins. I did not feel this need until I
> had my first child. When I first saw my son I wept because
> he was the first living being I had ever seen to whom I
> was truly related. It was an overwhelming experience, a
> kind of total system-shock. I say this so you will know
> that this is not usually a teenage identity crisis. A large
> proportion of us in this position are in our 30s and 40s. I
> do not need a new mother, I've got a wonderful one of
> my own. I do not need a new family, mine is the best
> there is. I can never, however, expect to find the warm
> relation of my fantasies and I know it. What is it I want
> then? If you are not adopted, you cannot know what it is
> to be shut out of a family's history.**

searches until after their adoptive parents' death. Others may find it hard to talk with their parents in case they cause pain or distress. On the other hand, some adoptive parents feel sad that they may be left out of their adopted son or daughter's search for their birth parents after being so intimately involved in their formative years. With greater openness now this is another area for sensitivity in sharing.

How will you feel?

It's important for you to try not to see any interest your child might have in his or her birth parents as a threat to his or her relationship with you. Try to put yourself in their place. Wouldn't you be intrigued to know what your birth mother was like – what she looked like and how she felt about you? Or to find out a bit more about your father? It's a natural instinct and much the best way for you to deal with it is to be as positive as possible.

You know more about your child than anyone and you can help them. If you say something like: 'When you're 18 you can get your birth certificate and if you want to trace your birth parents I can help you,' your son or daughter will involve you and won't

As many others who were adopted would agree, the need for truth and identity grows deeper with the years. That curiosity fluctuates between 'Well, I wasn't wanted then so why should now be any different?' and 'That's a chance I've got to take'. At various stages during my life I'd given very deep thought to the situation, particularly on my twenty-first birthday. Anyway, last year, with our four children all teenagers, I felt that my husband and I could at least spend a little of our spare time on the search. A little...? That's a laugh! It took over our lives! My whole family was behind me in this venture and I feel sure I would not have managed without their support. My one big regret is not being able to confide in my adoptive mother. Over the years any questions from me resulted in tears and obvious distress, so I felt it would be unkind to say anything. Now of course I feel very guilty.

feel embarrassed (as many do) or that they are being unfair to you. You won't run the risk, as many adopters have, of not being told that your adopted son or daughter is trying to trace their birth parents. But if, however positive you are, your son or daughter still feels uneasy and decides to leave you out or to discuss the search with someone else rather than you, try not to feel hurt. It can be a very difficult emotional time for him or her. Having more than one set of parents is confusing. And remember, too, that the birth parent has had a real influence on the way your child has developed over the years, despite being absent, and he or she has a right to find out more about that influence, if they choose. This does not mean that they are rejecting or devaluing all the parenting and love you have given them over many years (the 'What is a parent?' box in Chapter 10 might help).

It is very important to point out that adopters, however supportive they are, can feel irrationally but nonetheless painfully hurt when a reunion actually occurs. Many have told us this and were not expecting it. Remember, it's OK to feel this and it may be useful to talk to another adoptive parent or counsellor.

Talking to children at different ages and stages: one family's experience

Right from the beginning we built up a loose leaf album with special photographs – Peter as a tiny baby, one we fortunately had of Janet, his birth mother, visits to his foster home, his first day with us, special events together, the celebration tea we had when his adoption order was granted.

Sometimes when he was very young, cuddled up together after a bath looking at picture books, we would look at Peter's album mostly pointing out colours and naming things, but also each time talking of Janet as his "first" mum, saying he grew from a tiny egg in her tummy before he came to live with us and be adopted.

Of course we showed great pleasure in the photograph of the day he was adopted. When he was small each year we had a special cake at teatime on that date and grandma and grandpa joined us. We looked at the album again then. If we heard of someone who was adopted we might say, 'how nice, just like you'.

From about three, Peter really liked reading stories especially with lots of repetition. We added words to the photograph album – just very simply like – 'This is Peter, and here is Janet. Peter grew from a tiny egg in her tummy. Janet wanted Peter to be happy but she did not have a home for him. Peter went to stay with Auntie Sarah just for a little while. He was a very good baby but got lots of hiccups. Janet wanted Peter to have a new mummy and daddy who would love him and look after him. She heard about Anne and Derek (us!) and thought they sounded just right for Peter. Anne and Derek were so excited. They were so sad when they could not grow a baby themselves... now they could adopt Peter. Anne and Derek jumped into their blue car and went to Auntie Sarah's house to see Peter. He was wearing...'.

I don't know how much he understood but we put in lots of sound effects and different voices for sad and excited and we read it lots of times. Sometimes he would want to read it every night for a week – then he would be on to something else. Sometimes he would ask questions, mostly simple factual things. Some we had to be careful about – like when he said he did not like Janet's hair and hoped he'd have hair like mine!

Other events could spark questions – like when a close family friend was pregnant and he wondered who would adopt her baby! Sorting that out led him to ask more about why Janet didn't keep him. As he was a bit older then, about six and a half, we could tell him more about Janet's problems – like the fact that as a teenager she had lots of rows with her mum and step-dad and eventually she left home, but she had no job, she wouldn't ask them to help, and she stayed with various friends. She had a boyfriend called Jason who was Peter's first dad. We tried to emphasise that while Janet's life was in a bit of a mess when Peter was born, she did care about him and wanted the best for him. We explained that sometimes Janet didn't have enough money to buy his milk, or other times she was so tired she was frightened she would fall asleep and not hear him cry when it was time for his feed. Once he surprised us by wondering if Janet would know about his part in the school play – and then asking if we could tell her. We chose a nice photograph together and wrote about what he was doing (including the play!) and sent it all to our adoption agency for her if she should get in touch with them.

When we adopted our second child there was another burst of questions – particularly comparing first visits – like was he the same size as his new sister when we saw him first. There were more questions about why we could not have babies. He saw different people visiting and as we explained about the court, he checked out that once the judge decided, he really belonged in our family.

Once Peter was about eight or nine there seemed to be times when he worried more about Janet. Sometimes we would find him looking thoughtfully at her photograph. He would wonder what she was doing now. Obviously we could not answer but we told him more about what we knew. This included explaining that when she was unhappy she had started taking drugs as she hoped this would make things better but it didn't. He had already been asking us some questions about that with all the mention of drugs on the TV. Sometimes we would be able to talk easily together, at other times he would act as though he couldn't care less or tell us to shut up as he didn't want to talk about it.

Peter's school covers sex education at about age 10. This seemed to spark off questions about his first dad – and we knew very little about Jason. Again we tried writing to our adoption agency. They sent us a letter including all the information they had but I think Peter would have liked more.

The teenager years were full of the usual ups and downs and different moods. Occasionally we would have really good chats round the kitchen table. Sometimes talking about the common adolescent concerns – behaviour and pressure from the others at school (particularly when a couple of older boys were suspended for having drugs), sex and girl friends and later on contraception – plus of course all the hopes and fears for the future of the sort of adult he would be, we wondered if being adopted made a big difference. Sometimes during rows Peter would shout, 'You can't tell me what to do – you're not my real parents anyway'. The first time this happened we were stunned and really hurt and asked ourselves, 'What have we done wrong?' However, we soon realised that what Peter was really doing was asking, 'Who am I? Am I the product of Janet and Jason or of you two, or a

mixture of both?' The next time this happened we just said, quite
calmly, 'We're not your birth parents, we wish we were because
we're proud of you and love you so much. But if you had been
born to us we might have missed out because you wouldn't be
the special person you are!' A few times Peter actually made the
connection with Janet or brought up questions about his
adoption – who he would be like, what he might have inherited
from her or Jason and how much he would be like us. At other
times we were aware of the links and that we were in sensitive
areas but didn't want to make a big issue of it. There were also,
however, periods when he just did not want to talk with us and
would be very offhand or spend all his time in his room.

It would of course have to be at one of these times when a letter
arrived from our adoption agency out of the blue saying that
Janet had contacted them. She was delighted with the earlier
photographs of Peter and would be happy if he wanted to get in
touch in the future – she now had her life more in order. It did
not seem a good time to tell Peter – but if we didn't we could
equally be in trouble with him for not letting him know. In the
end we told him about the letter and he just shrugged it off and
wouldn't say anything. We did write back to the adoption agency
so Janet wouldn't be left wondering what happened.

We were all thrilled when at the age of 18, Peter got a place at
university. We all went out for a celebration dinner and over a
cup of coffee afterwards he suddenly said he would like to let
Janet know. He wrote a note the next day and a couple of weeks
later a congratulations card came back from Janet via the
adoption agency. Peter is clear that at the moment that is
enough for him. He wants to concentrate on his life at university.
He thinks they might exchange cards and bits of information and
maybe meet sometime in the future.

Useful organisations

Parent to Parent Information on Adoption Services (PPIAS)

PPIAS is a national organisation for adoptive parents, their children and those hoping to adopt. There are over 140 volunteer co-ordinators scattered throughout the country and most of these hold meetings where a wide variety of topics related to adoption, including telling, can be discussed and there is the opportunity to meet people in similar circumstances. PPIAS members include many types of adoptive family, from those who have adopted healthy babies to those who have enlarged their family with one or more older or disabled child. People intending to adopt can also join, as one of the best ways of finding out what adopting involves is to talk to people who've already done it.

Local groups usually hold some family events such as summer picnics, Christmas parties, etc, where children can meet other adopted children. From a child's point of view it's very comforting to have some friends who are adopted. It makes the whole thing seem more normal and less 'different', and it gives children the opportunity to share similar feelings and experiences. They enjoy going to the picnics and meeting their friends. Knowing other adoptive families with new children and babies arriving keeps the subject near the surface and discussable. PPIAS produce a quarterly journal, *Adoption UK*, full of fascinating experiences of adopters and adopted people.

Parent to Parent Information on Adoption Services is at:

Lower Boddington, Daventry, Northants
NN11 6YB Tel. 01327 260295

It's worth joining just to read this. They also provide a range of
further information packs and leaflets on specific topics and
have a Resource Bank through which adopters can share similar
experiences.

To find out about other locally based self-help/support groups for
adoptive parents you can contact your adoption agency or local
authority social services department or social work department.

The National Organisation for Counselling Adoptees and their Parents (NORCAP)

NORCAP is a support group that offers the opportunity to talk to
people who have had similar experiences. There are many
'contact leaders' around the country.

NORCAP aims to help and counsel: adopted people who are
thinking of searching for their birth parents – it will suggest
ideas and viewpoints to be considered before making a decision
which will have far-reaching consequences; birth parents who
either long for, or dread, a contact from the past – they can be
put in touch with others in the same position; adoptive parents
whose lives will be affected by any search their adopted children
may start – it offers reassurance that they are only trying to find
out more about themselves, and can provide information on
ways of answering their child's questions. NORCAP encourages
the use of intermediaries in making any contact. NORCAP also
has a small group interested in the particular needs of
'foundlings'. Members receive a newsletter three times per year
and can buy other publications.

NORCAP is at:

112 Church Road
Wheatley
Oxon OX33 1LU
Tel: 01865 875000

| **Post and After Adoption Centres**

There are many well established after adoption services now that provide support for adoptive families, adopted people and birth parents whose children were adopted. Many of them offer counselling, preferably in person, but also on the telephone or by correspondence, for individuals and families. Some also organise events which focus on matters related to adoption, and provide the opportunity for people to meet in common interest groups. Some, like the Post-Adoption Centre in London, arrange a periodic programme of workshops to help parents explore some of the issues involved in communicating with children about adoption and to consider new ideas and approaches. A growing number of local authority social services / work departments and voluntary adoption agencies provide post-adoption services.

Post-Adoption Centre
5 Torriano Mews
Torriano Ave
London NW5 2RZ
Tel. 0171 284 0555

ATRAP (Association of Transracially Adopted People)
c/o Post-Adoption Centre
(see above)

After Adoption
12-14 Chapel Street
Salford
Manchester M3 7NN
Tel. 0161 839 4930

After Adoption Yorkshire & Humberside
82 Cardigan Road
Leeds LS6 3BT
Tel. 0113 2302100

After Adoption Wales
Unit 1
Cowbridge Court
58-62 Cowbridge Road
West Cardiff CF5 5BS
Tel. 01222 575711

West Midlands Post-Adoption Service (WMPAS)
92 Newcombe Road
Handsworth
Birmingham
B21 8DD
Tel. 0121 523 3343

Merseyside Adoption Centre
316-317 Coopers Building
Church Street
Liverpool L1 3AA
Tel. 0151 709 9122

Adoption Counselling Centre
Family Care
21 Castle Street
Edinburgh
EH2 3DN
Tel. 0131 225 6441

Barnardo's Scottish Adoption Advice Centre
16 Sandyford Place
Glasgow G3 7NB
Tel. 0141 339 0772

British Agencies for Adoption and Fostering (BAAF)

BAAF is a registered charity and professional association for all those working in the child care field. BAAF's work includes: giving advice and information to members of the public on aspects of adoption, fostering and child care issues; publishing a wide range of books, training packs and leaflets as well as a quarterly journal on adoption, fostering and child care issues; providing training and consultancy services to social workers and other professionals to help them improve the quality of medical, legal and social work services to children and families; giving evidence to government committees on subjects concerning children and families; responding to consultative documents on changes in legislation and regulations affecting children in or at risk of coming into care; and helping to find new families for children through BAAF*Link* and Be My Parent.

More information about BAAF can be obtained from our offices listed below.

Head Office
Skyline House
200 Union Street
London SE1 0LX
Tel. 0171 593 2000

Be My Parent
Tel. 0171 593 2060
(At Head Office)

Scottish Centre
40 Shandwick Place
Edinburgh EH2 4RT
Tel. 0131 225 9285

Welsh Centre
7 Cleeve House
Lambourne Crescent
Cardiff CF4 5GJ
Tel. 01222 761155

Central and Northern Region
St. George's House
Coventry Road
Coleshill
Birmingham B46 3EA
Tel. 01675 463998

and at:
Grove Villa
82 Cardigan Road
Headingley
Leeds LS6 3BJ
Tel. 0113 274 4797

and at:
MEA House
Ellison Place
Newcastle-upon-Tyne
NE1 8XS
Tel. 0191 261 6600

BAAF*Link*
Tel. 0191 232 3200
(At Newcastle Office)

Southern Region
Skyline House
200 Union Street
London SE1 0LX
Tel. 0171 593 2041/42

and at:
PO Box 128
Bristol
Westbury-on-Trym BS9 3AB

Other useful organisations

The National Stepfamily Association is the national organisation providing information, support and advice for all members of stepfamilies and those who work with them.
Chapel House, 18 Hatton Place,
London EC1N 8RU
Tel. 0171 209 2460

The Overseas Adoption Helpline deals with general aspects of overseas adoption for all of the UK.
PO Box 13899
London N6 4WB
Tel. 0990 168742

Useful books

Please note that some of the books mentioned below may be out of print but your library may have copies available or be able to obtain the book you require.

Books for adopted children and young people

Books from BAAF

Children's book series, BAAF 1997, 1998.
A new and unique series of books for use with children separated from their birth parents. The stories are simply told and attractively illustrated in full colour. Worksheets at the back of each workbook will help children to compare and contrast their own experiences with those of the characters in the story.

Living with a new family: Nadia and Rashid's story
Nadia is ten and Rashid seven. When their father died some years ago, their birth mother, Pat, found it hard to look after them. So Nadia and Rashid went to live with Jenny, a foster carer, and then with their new parents, Ayesha and Azeez.

Belonging doesn't mean forgetting: Nathan's story
Nathan is a four-year-old African-Caribbean boy and has just started school. His birth mum, Rose, found it hard to be a good mum and wanted someone else to look after him. Nathan went to live with foster carers Tom and Delores. And then with Marlene, her daughter Sophie, Grannie and Aunty Bea.

Hoping for the best: Jack's story
Jack is an eight-year-old white boy. His birth mum, Maria, couldn't look after him because she was unhappy and unwell. Jack went to live with Peter and Sarah. At first he was happy but then started to feel sad and mixed up. Peter and Sarah did not think they could be the right mum and dad for him and Jack had to leave.

Jo's story (forthcoming)
Tomorrow will be a big day for eight-year-old Joanne. She is going to court with her mum, stepfather and baby brother to be adopted. Jo knows that although Dave isn't her birth father he wants to help look after her for the rest of her life.

Feeling safe: Tina's story (forthcoming)
Tina wasn't safe at home and now lives with Molly who is her foster carer. Tina had to move after she told a teacher about how her Dad's touches made her feel bad. She is not sure whether she will ever be able to live with her family again but feels safe with her foster family.

Lidster A, *Chester and Daisy Move On*, BAAF, 1995.
A delightful picture book about two bear cubs who go to live with a foster family and are then prepared to move to an adoptive family. For use with four to ten-year-olds.

Sparks K, *Why Adoption?*, BAAF, 1995.
Experiences to share for teenagers and their adoptive parents – adoption as seen from a young person's perspective.

Books from other publishers

Althea, *My New Family*, Dinosaur (in conjunction with NFCA), 1984.
A school-aged girl moves from a children's home to a foster home where she can remain as long as she wants and where she is clearly becoming part of the family. Covers areas like the role of the social worker, life story books, settling in and understanding that even loving families have rows!

Bond M, *The Paddington Books*, Collins.
These books are well known to most children but remember that Paddington has to get used to living in a family for the first time. He has brought with him from Peru his scrapbook, a photo of his Aunt Lucy, and little else. He settles down in his new home despite many traumatic experiences but often thinks back to his past.

Edwards D and Dinan C, *Robert Goes to Fetch a Sister*, Methuen, 1986.
A story of transracial adoption for young children between the ages of three to seven. Robert, adopted as a baby, listens again to his own story and goes with his parents to collect a new baby.

Frendberg J and Geiss T, *Susan and Gordon Adopt a Baby*, Random House, 1986.
Based on the American TV series *Sesame Street*, this is the story of black parents who adopt a baby, aided (or hampered) by the puppet Big Bird. It can be used to help explain adoption to a young (four to seven year old) child.

Keller H, *Red Fox*, Picture Books, 1993.
An animal story for young children. Every night Horace's mother tells him that they chose him because he lost his first family and needed a new one. They liked his spots – but the rest of the family have stripes! The book describes Horace's search for a family where he "belongs", and who also have spots. At the end of the day he goes back home and tells his mama 'If you chose me, can I choose you too?'

McAfee A and Browne A, *The Visitors who Came to Stay*, Hamish Hamilton, 1984.
Kate lives alone with her dad. Life changes when Mary and her son Sean become regular visitors. An unusual and amusing book with remarkable illustrations.

Miller K A, *Did My First Mother Love Me?*, Morning Glory Press, 1994, USA.
A story for an adopted child with a special section for adoptive parents. In the story Moyan has a letter from her birth mother which she needs to read with her adoptive mother; she then wonders: did my first mother love me?

My Story, Infertility Research Trust, University Dept of Obstetrics and Gynaecology, Jessop Hospital for Women, 1991.
Not specifically on adoption but useful to look at when talking to children about assisted reproduction. This book was written by two mothers of children born by donor insemination who wanted to be honest with their children in telling them how they were conceived. The aim of the book is to help other families in this position to put their thoughts into words.

Nystram C, *Andy's Big Question*, Lion Books, 1987.
This is part of a Christian based series. Andy is a boy of mixed parentage who joins a busy family at the age of three. He is adopted by them and there are two birth children and foster children who come and go. Andy is now 10 and the book explores some of the questions and concerns he has.

Snell N, *Steve is Adopted*, Hamish Hamilton, 1985.
Steve is a little black boy adopted into a white family. He feels 'it's nice to feel wanted'. This story book could be used with small children asking about adoption and being black in a white family (he is described in the book as being "brown").

Wilson J, *The Story of Tracy Beaker*, Yearling Books 1992.
Tracy is 10 years old. She lives in a Children's Home but would like a real home one day. Written as Tracy's diary this is a lively humorous book which reveals a lot of what goes on in the minds of children separated from their parents. As she says herself, 'I'm Tracy Beaker. This is a book about all about me. I'd read it if I were you. It's the most incredible, dynamic, heart-rending story. Honest!'

Wright S, *Real Sisters*, Ragweed, 1994.
What is a real sister anyway? This is the question seven-year-old Claire must answer for herself when classmates in the school yard taunt her. Because Claire is adopted they say that her older sister Jenny is not her real sister. This booklet takes a realistic look at what it means to be a sister. Claire is of mixed parentage, her sister white.

| **Novels for teenagers**

Ashley B, *The Trouble with Donovan Croft*, Puffin, 1984.
This is a story about an African-Caribbean boy fostered in a white family. Donovan is unhappy he couldn't speak. This book is about trying to find out ways of reaching this very confused boy – and the relationship between Donovan and his white foster brother.

Blackman B, *Hacker*, Corgi, 1992.
At the beginning of this book Vicki, adopted as a baby, isn't exactly best pals with her brother who was born into the family! But when her adoptive father is arrested and accused of stealing over a million pounds from the bank, she is thrust into an adventure with her brother trying to prove her father's innocence. The ending not only solves the crime but it also establishes the relationship between Vicki and her brother and how she belongs in the family.

Leach B, *Anna Who?*, Attic Press, 1994, Eire.
Anna's adopted. When she was little her mother used to call her "our special daughter". But now Anna is 14 and she doesn't feel so special anymore. All Anna wants to do is to get away from her family and discover who she really is. But then something happens and Anna slowly begins to realise that she doesn't need to know where she came from to know who she is.

Lowry L, *Find a Stranger, Say Goodbye*, Viking Kestrel Books. 1980.
The story of an adopted girl's search for her birth mother. Everything is going well in her present family but she needs to know her background. She carries out her

searching in a responsible way and the feelings it stirs up are realistic. Eventually she finds her birth mother and returns to her adoptive family who she discovers to be her "real" parents.

Nerlove E, *Who is David?* Child Welfare League of America Inc, 1985, USA.
An involving story that should capture the attention of many adopted adolescents, especially boys. David struggles with his curiosity about his original parents in a happy adoptive home. His emerging friendship with Diana is sensitively described.

Noel D, *Five to Seven: The story of a 1920s childhood*, Robin Clark, 1980.
A small girl copes with the terrors of life caused by unpredictable adults, and separation from the key figure in her life.

Paterson K, *The Great Gilly Hopkins*, Puffin 1984.
Gilly Hopkins is a tough operator – she's super cool and super intelligent. And she's not going to be had by anyone: teacher, social worker or foster parent. All she wants is a reunion with her beautiful long-lost mother. But just when it appears her dream might come true things no longer seem quite so clear cut.

Pearce P, *The Way to Satin Shore*, Viking Kestrel, 1983.
Kate's family refuse to tell her about her dead father. They do not understand that until she finds out the truth about her father she cannot cope with living in the present.

Note: Children's books are regularly reviewed in *Adoption UK*, the newsletter published by PPIAS (see Useful Organisations for details).

| **Books for adults**

Books from BAAF

Adopting a Child: a guide for people interested in adoption, BAAF, 1998.
Essential reading for anyone who is considering adopting a child and very useful for existing adoptive parents, this down-to-earth guide gives clear and up-to-date information on all stages of the adoption process. It includes names and addresses of adoption and fostering agencies throughout the country, with maps showing their location, and details of other organisations concerned with adoption.

Howe D, *Adopters on Adoption: Reflections on parenthood and children*, BAAF 1996.
This absorbing collection of personal stories of adoptive parents covers topics including assessment and preparation, feelings towards birth mothers and biology, infertility and parenting secure children.

McNamara J, Bullock A, Grimes E, *Bruised Before Birth*, BAAF, 1995.
This book contains invaluable tools, suggestions and resources which will enable child care professionals and adoptive parents and foster carers to meet the complex needs that a substance-exposed infant or child may manifest.

McWhinnie A and Batty D, *Children of Incest: Whose secret is it?*, BAAF, 1993.
This book explores the key issues that arise in telling someone born of incest the truth about their origins. Supported by case histories.

Mullender A and Kearn S, *I'm Here Waiting: Birth relatives' views on Part II of the Adoption Contact Register for England and Wales*, BAAF, 1997.
This study explores the views of birth relatives on the Register and highlights the anomolies created by current legislation.

Phillips R and McWilliam E, *After Adoption, Working with adoptive families*, BAAF, 1996.
This unique anthology, illustrated with case studies, focuses on post-adoption support for adoptive families.

Ryan T, and Walker R, *Life Story Work*, BAAF, 1993.
An invaluable guide to the innovative and imaginative techniques now available to help children come to terms with their painful pasts. It outlines the background theory and offers practical suggestions for using games and projects like family trees, maps and life graphs that aid the healing process. Illustrated with drawings and photographs.

Books from other publishers

Surviving Five, Barnardo's, 1993.
This short very readable book gives an insight into how one family coped with the different needs of a family of five brothers and sisters from introductions through the first year of placement. It shows some of the issues that need to be addressed with children at different ages and stages.

Bernstein A C, *Flight of the Stork: What Children think (and when) about sex and family building*, Perspectives Press, 1994, USA.
An expansion of an earlier book on talking to children about sex recognising their needs and what they understand at different stages of development. The new edition includes chapters on children born as a result of assisted reproduction and those growing up in adoptive and stepfamilies.

Charlton L, Crank M, Kansara K, Oliver C, *Still Screaming: Birth parents compulsorily separated from their children*, After Adoption, 1998. This book provides revealing and hard-hitting accounts of what birth parents think and feel when their children are adopted against their wishes.

Preparing For Reunion, The Children's Society, 1998.
Adopted people, adoptive parents and birth parents tell their stories. This book addresses many of the commonly asked questions like When should I search? What am I letting myself in for? Am I being disloyal? Should I keep this secret? Do I really need counselling?

Howe D, Sawbridge P, Hinings D, *Half a Million Women*, The Post-Adoption Centre, 1997.
This book examines aspects of the experience of giving up a child for adoption.

Jones M, *Everything you Need to Know about Adoption*, Sheldon House (SPCK), 1987.
A very useful guide to adoption with plenty of quotations from people who've "done it". Includes material on transracial and intercountry adoption.

Kay J, *The Adoption Papers*, Bloodaxe Books, 1991.
Jackie Kay has been gathering a reputation for her talent in poetry and play writing. She was also adopted transracially by a white Scottish couple. *The Adoption Papers* is her first collection of poetry, the major part of which expresses through that medium the different viewpoints of the mother, the birth mother, and the daughter.

Krementz J, *How it Feels to be Adopted*, Victor Gollancz, 1984.
The views of 19 adopted young people in the USA, ranging in age from 8 to 16 years old. It could be read by adults or children and reflects many of the feelings children have about their adoption.

Post-Adoption Centre, *A Glimpse through the Looking Glass*, 1990.
A discussion paper that examines issues of relevance to transracially adopted black adults.

Rosenberg E B, *The Adoption Life Cycle*, The Free Press, 1992.
A readable book which combines current research theory and practical advice relevant to all those directly involved in the adoption experience – adopters, adoptive parents and birth parents, as well as professionals. It provides a framework for understanding the important developmental tasks which span the lifetimes of those involved.

Tugendhat J, *The Adoption Triangle*, Bloomsbury, 1992.
What happens when adopted people wish to search for their lost families? This book includes interviews with many adopted adults, birth parents, and adoptive parents and those professionally involved. Starting from looking at the particular perspectives of birth mother, birth father, adopted individual and adoptive parents, it goes on to explore both the search and reunions.

Wells S, *Within me, Without me*, Scarlet Press, 1994.
This collection of personal stories explores the experiences of mothers who have given up children for adoption.

Note: Books for adults are regularly reviewed in *Adoption and Fostering*, BAAF's journal and in *Adoption UK*, the newsletter published by PPIAS (see Useful Organisations for details).

| Leaflets from BAAF

Adoption – Some questions answered
Basic information about adoption – the process, procedures, the law and useful resources.

If you are adopted
Answers to some of the questions adopted children ask, aimed at the children themselves. Includes information on tracing birth parents.

Intercountry Adoption – Information and guidance
Information on adopting a child from overseas, including procedures, legislation, and where to obtain advice and further information.

Stepchildren and Adoption (separate editions for England & Wales and Scotland)
Information on Stepfamilies, the advantages or not of adoption, the alternatives and
obtaining further advice.

Talking about Origins
An outline of adopted children's need to be told about adoption and the law on
access to birth certificates.

For further reading

Articles regularly appear in BAAF's quarterly journal, *Adoption & Fostering*, which
may be of interest to adoptive parents. For subscription details, contact BAAF.